MORE TIME,
LESS STRESS

Contents

Introduction

When I joined the tutorial staff at Ashridge Management College I had no experience as a teacher or trainer. The College very kindly put me on its four-week 'General Management Programme', known colloquially as the 'G' course, as a participant. I spent an exciting month simultaneously listening to the content and observing the process. Who were the most effective tutors? How did they do it?

My chief conclusion was that, when you walk into a room to work with a group of 36 people, you are on stage and you must put on a performance. There are many different styles of performance and all tutors must develop their own, but the worst sin is to be boring.

I suspect that the same is true of a book, and have attempted to use humour, example and analogy to help the reader through these pages.

WHO SHOULD READ THIS BOOK?

Anyone who is short of time and feels stressed by it. Since I have been running Time Management courses with and for managers, they must be the primary audience, though I hope there will be plenty in it for others. Indeed the principles discussed apply to many areas of life, and in some chapters I have highlighted 'lessons for life'.

My own interest in time management arose because I was bad at it. Like many who work in newspapers or other industries with constant short-term pressures, I had an uneasy feeling that I was not really in control.

In 1983 I was made programme director of the 'G' course, responsible, among other things, for the course content. In November of that year, in the introductory session to one course, several participants mentioned time management as a particular problem. Since the subject was not included in the programme I offered to develop a short session and run it as an optional extra in the fourth week. With the additional motivation of this deadline I prepared my first session, and it has been with me ever since.

Most time management books have been written by highly organized people, and are full of crisp little pearls of wisdom like 'Handle each piece of paper only once' – a worthy objective, but not really very helpful. This book is not so prescriptive. It explores the reasons for time problems and attempts to provoke and prod the reader into self-analysis. It is, therefore, a book for disorganized managers. I believe that we teach best what we most need to learn and I confess that much of what I have written is from personal experience. I come from a disorganized past.

TOTAL QUALITY TIME

Among the most exciting developments in the past 20 years has been the concept of Total Quality Management.

It is generally reckoned that the cost of poor quality in traditional manufacturing operations amounts to about 20 or 30 per cent of total costs. This would include all scrap, rework, chasing, checking, expediting etc. – in other words all the costs that would not be incurred if all operations were carried out correctly, first time and every time.

This used to be accepted as a fact of life: 'We're only human', 'You must allow a margin for error', 'You can't win them all', etc. Total Quality Management challenges this. It is based on the assumption that it is possible to get it right every time – total quality.

In service businesses, the cost of poor quality is often as great as 40 per cent of total costs.

What is the personal cost to you of poor quality? What proportion of your time do you spend searching for things, chasing, checking, apologizing, handling complaints, problems and crises – and doing anything that would not have been necessary if everyone produced total quality all the time? This is a frightening question for many managers, because it describes much of their traditional work.

Total quality must start with clear requirements. How can anyone know whether they have got it right if they don't know what 'right' means? In this way quality is always defined in the customer's terms. Total quality also involves everyone in evaluating their own work, their systems and their products, continually searching for improvements.

Many of us have a subsconscious mind-set from childhood of the world as a stable place, in which 'change' is an occasional irritation. Total quality seeks to replace this with the concept of continuous improvement – or 'kaizen' as the Japanese call it – in which everyone knows that next month *they* will do a better job than this month, that tomorrow *they* will do a better job than today; and everyone knows that it is up to *them* to make this happen.

This book is about continuous improvement. It invites you to analyse your own requirements, to reflect on your systems and procedures and to develop strategies for doing a better job in the future.

It is also about reducing stress. We feel stressed when we are responsible for something but not in control of it. If you are not in control of your time you are likely to be feeling an undercurrent of stress in your life.

I would like to thank members of G883 for the original stimulus, and also the many thousands of managers I have worked with whose participation has made every session different and who, between them, have built up my understanding of the problems, and some of the answers.

I am also indebted to those who have gone before and from whose writings I have learned, to many people who have helped in the production of this book and particularly to my friend Peter Allen for his delightful drawings.

PART I
WHAT ARE THE PROBLEMS?

Time management is like slimming. Many people know they need it and frequently buy books on the subject.

The first section of this book looks at the problems most frequently mentioned as causing poor time management and offers simple advice on overcoming them. The key chapters in this section are chapter 1, *What is time management?* and chapter 2, *Priorities* – the key to effective time management.

1. What is Time Management?

Time is a valuable resource. Time passes inexorably in a fixed rhythm: 60 seconds every minute, 60 minutes every hour. Time which has passed can never come back. Time is a democratically shared resource: we all have 24 hours every day, seven days every week. It doesn't matter how wealthy you are, you can't buy more time. You can't hoard time, borrow time, steal time or change it in any way. All you can do is *make the best use of the time you have*. Of all the resources we have, time seems to be the least understood and the most mismanaged. Wherever I go I hear people saying they don't have enough time, yet everyone has all the time there is.

We don't always experience time in the same way. Time seems to move slowly when you are bored, unoccupied, or particularly impatient for something to happen – consider the length of a minute when you are waiting for a kettle to boil, a traffic light to turn green, a telephone to be answered, or a computer system to give you access. Time seems to move fast when you are busy, interested and having a good time.

Time also seems to accelerate. If you take a two-week holiday, the second week goes faster than the first. The same is true of a management course and, I am afraid, of a lifetime; the second half goes faster than the first. It has something to do with our sense of perspective. At the age of 15, a year is a very long time. Now, for many of us, the years are passing by rather faster.

If that last comment caused you to wince, then good. If you are looking for a relaxing bedtime book to send you to sleep, try Jeffrey Archer: this book is intended to wake you up. John Cleese once said that he measured the success of his Video Arts films by their 'squirm factor' – the same goes for this book. If it makes you wince occasionally in self-recognition then it is doing its job.

Maybe the best way to get into the subject of time is to think of yourself in a time perspective. Think of yourself as you were in the past, and then peer into the future. Take a specific time, about five years ago, and try to get a clear mental picture of yourself as you were at that time, using the following questions to help you. Five years ago:

How old were you?
What did you look like?
What did you wear?
Where did you live?
Were you married?
Did you have children? If so, how old were they?
What sports did you play?
Where did you take your holiday?
What job were you doing?
What have you achieved in the past five years?
How fast have they passed?

Five years is not a long time, is it? It has passed quite quickly. The most difficult question for most people is the next to last one. What have you achieved in the past five years?

Now for the future. It is difficult looking ahead and there are no certainties, but it is important to try. Given the apparent acceleration of time, with each year going faster than the one before, I am going to ask you to look ten years ahead to get a proper balance, again with the help of some questions. Ten years ahead:

How old will you be?
What will you look like?
Where will you live?
How old will your children be?
What job will you be doing?
What would you like to do before then?

That wasn't very nice, was it? But it might be important. In fact it is so important that I want you to write down a few answers to the last question. Time management must be about life, not just about work, but for the moment I suggest you confine your thoughts to work and career. Ten years is too far away for realistic plans, so let me reframe the question: What do you want to do, in the context of your work and your career, in the next 12 months?

In the next 12 months I want to:

. . . .
. . . .
. . . .

Now consider this scenario. Next time you are at work, the boss calls you in – not your boss, but The Boss, The Big Chief in your organization. 'How are you? Did you have a good weekend? I have a request to put to you. There is a project I would like you to undertake. It is of vital importance to the future of this organization. It will take about a year, working approximately one day a week. It will involve some overseas travel and, because it is so important, I want you to report directly to me for your work on this project. Unfortunately there is one slight snag: I cannot release you from your present responsibilities. Is there any chance you could undertake this project for me in addition to your present job?'

Would you accept? I suspect that, for most people, the word 'Yes' would appear somewhere in the answer to this. Some would say 'Yes please'. Others would say 'Yes if . . .' or 'Yes but . . .' and not everybody would say yes.

By saying 'yes', you are saying that *you do have time . . . if something is important enough.* How important are the objectives you set down for the next 12 months? If they are important enough you can find time for them.

Many people claim that lack of time is a big problem, until they come to the nasty realization that it is not a problem, it is a symptom, a symptom of unclear objectives, of poor allocation of priorities and poor planning.

Maybe the title of this book ought to be *Setting Objectives and Deciding Priorities*, but that would be boring.

For many years I have frequently been asked to run seminars on 'Time Management' and never, even once, have I been asked to run a session on 'Setting Objectives and Deciding Priorities'. Yet that must be the central theme. 'Time Management' is a catchy title. It sells courses, but it is a nonsense title if you stop to think about it: you cannot manage time. Time passes inexorably in a fixed rhythm: 60 seconds every minute, 60 minutes every hour . . . there is nothing you can do about that. In fact there is only one thing you can manage, and that is yourself. 'Self Management' is the real title of this work. It is about YOU, the way you do your job and the way you live your life.

If that is so, then devices and gimmicks to save minutes will not solve anything. Time management is not about *speed*, it is about *effectiveness*.

So how do you manage yourself? What is it that stops you being more effective? Switch your brain into active mode and write down whatever you can think of that inhibits your effectiveness at work.

The material for this book has been developed on management courses, where the sessions are participative, so I shall invite readers to participate from time to time. You may prefer to whizz on at top speed: that's your choice. But the book is more likely to prove helpful to you, and to the way you do your job, if you contribute your own perceptions.

What are your time-wasters at work?

What stops you being more effective?

TIME-WASTERS

. . . .
. . . .
. . . .
. . . .
. . . .
. . . .
. . . .
. . . .
. . . .
. . . .
. . . .
. . . .
. . . .
. . . .

On the next page is a typical list generated by managers attending a seminar. Though far from complete, it probably bears some similarity to the list you have produced.

TIME-WASTERS

INTERRUPTIONS
MEETINGS
TELEPHONE
CRISES AND PANICS
THE BOSS
FAULTY EQUIPMENT
CHASING PEOPLE
LACK OF RESOURCES
E-MAIL
JUNK MAIL
READING
FORM-FILLING
TRAVEL
SOCIAL CHAT

This is our menu. These are the problems I shall be looking at throughout this book. When I am running a seminar, as the day progresses, I always find some more time-wasters which were forgotten when the original list was compiled. That will probably happen to you as you read this book, so keep your original list in mind, add to it as we proceed and I shall update my list from time to time.

PEOPLE ARE DIFFERENT

We each have different characters, different backgrounds and do different jobs, so we do not all face the same problems and we do not all need the same answers. Indeed I shall not be offering 'The Answer' in this book. I shall write about common problems and ideas which people have found useful and I suggest that you treat the book as an 'à la carte' menu. If you don't like some of the ideas, or find them inappropriate to your situation, fine! Save some time by skipping on to the next item! If, by the end of the book, you have found two or three ideas which you can take away and use, then that should justify the cost of the book and your time spent reading it.

2. Priorities

I would like you to imagine some junior member of staff, let's call him Peter, doing a fairly simple job. Peter has 40 units of responsibility to discharge and achieves that in a 40-hour week. Everything is in balance and he can go home happy on Fridays, without a care in the world.

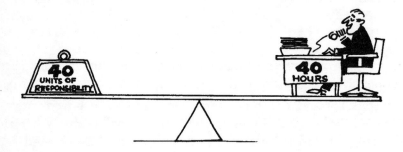

Now let us suppose that Peter is ambitious and wishes to progress. This progress will involve taking on more responsibility. Let us increase his responsibility to 60 units. Peter now has a dilemma. How can he get back into balance? He would appear to have two options: either he works a 60-hour week, or he finds some way of acquiring leverage.

There is no doubt which of these is the most sensible option. This leads me to suggest a simple principle: 'There is no correlation between the weight of organizational responsibility you carry and the amount of personal time needed to discharge that responsibility.' There cannot possibly be a correlation between responsibility and time. If there were, how could anyone be Chief Executive of Shell or President of France? The responsibility they carry is enormous in comparison with Peter's, or yours for that matter, and even for an insomniac workaholic there are only 168 hours in a week.

The answer to effectiveness is and always must be *leverage*. But what is leverage? What are the high-leverage parts of your present job? What things do you do where a little bit of effort now could make a big difference to your results in the long run? (I suggest you leave out negative items like 'Avoiding mistakes', important though that might be, and concentrate on active, positive tasks.)

My list would include the following:

PLANNING

This can include reviewing past performance, setting yourself objectives and planning for the future. It can be large scale or small; planning the month, planning the day, planning the meeting. But beware, planning is only of any value if it eventually translates into work. Planning which does not influence future action can be a complete waste of time – and there is plenty of that in many organizations.

SETTING UP SYSTEMS

These can be complex computer-based systems involving large numbers of people, or simple personal systems, like organizing your desk, but they are all designed to enable someone to handle routine tasks with less effort or better results in the future.

DELEGATION

Delegation also appears on the list, but if you were asked, at the end of a long hard day, 'What have you been doing today?' you would not answer 'Delegating'. We need to break delegation into its component parts. Delegation includes the setting and agreeing of objectives, gaining people's commitment to those objectives (which I take to include motivating them), and possibly some training.

LEARNING

This can be some skill or knowledge which can help you to be more effective in the future. Come to think of it, lack of training or skill could be said to be a time-waster which was inexplicably omitted from our earlier list. For example, many managers have keyboards on their desks but type with two fingers.

BUILDING AND MAINTAINING RELATIONSHIPS

These can be relationships with your boss, members of your own team, customers, suppliers, colleagues or anyone else who has a significant impact on your performance. Time spent building your relationship with such people can be a sound investment.

So my list looks like this:

High-leverage tasks
    Planning
    Setting up systems
    Delegation
    Learning
    Building and maintaining relationships

There might be one or two additions to this list, for example, recruitment in some cases, but these are the principal ones. These are the high-leverage activities which can make a big difference in the long run. Now pause and do some more thinking. In your last full week at work, what proportion of your time was actually spent working on these high-leverage tasks?

LAST WEEK

Time spent on high-leverage activities ... hours
Total time spent working ... hours
Percentage of working hours spent on high-leverage tasks ... %

PARETO'S LAW

You have probably heard of the 80/20 rule, originally propounded by the Italian economist Vilfredo Pareto. When applied to time at work it would state that: '20 per cent of the time at work is spent doing things which account for 80 per cent of the results and 80 per cent of the time is spent doing things which account for 20 per cent of the results'.

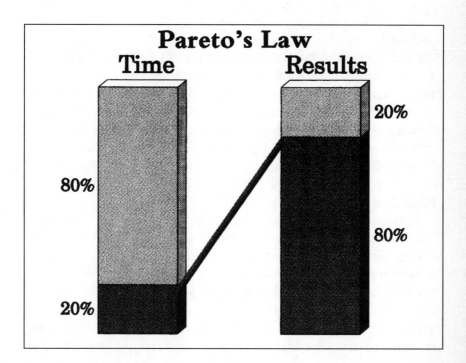

How did your week compare with that? Did you reach the Pareto average, 20 per cent of your time on high-leverage activities? Or was it rather less? For many, it is often a great deal less.

These are your high-leverage activities. This is where you could make a big difference to your effectiveness in the long run. They ought to be the focus of your energy and your time and yet you are almost ignoring them. Why?

This is where the subject of time management starts to get interesting. That bit about Peter on his see-saw was ridiculously simple: the answer was obvious. You didn't need a book to find that out. Yet many managers ignore the lesson. Why?

There are several traps that lie in wait for us — see if you recognise any of them.

WHAT IS IT THAT DISTRACTS US FROM PRIORITIES?

TRAP ONE: URGENCIES, CRISES AND PANICS

It is important for managers to realize that their job is never done — as a manager you can never be completely up to date. Your conscience will remind you of additional checks you might have made and your imagination will suggest possibilities you could have developed.

If at the end of the week you were to make two piles — one a pile of all the things you have done that week, the other a pile of all the things you might have done but haven't done — in which pile would the high-leverage tasks be? All too often they'd be sitting there waiting for next week . . . because they weren't urgent.

We are tyrannized by urgency. We do the urgent, and neglect the important. We let deadlines dictate our priorities. If jobs only get done when they become urgent you will live in a permanent state of crisis and stress.

High-leverage tasks tend to be to do with the long term, low-leverage to do with the short term. A classic example of a high-leverage activity is fire prevention; a classic example of a low-leverage activity is fire fighting.

Now this is the nub of the problem. If the building is on fire you know what you must do — but fire fighting is low-leverage. If all you ever do is fire fighting, you are not being effective. The real job is fire prevention. That is the high-leverage activity.

There will always be crises and panics, but every time a crisis arises I suggest there are two things you must do:

- First, deal with the immediate problem, put out the fire;
- Second, ask yourself: 'What can I do to make sure that type of crisis does not occur again?' Or, if it is totally beyond your control, ask yourself: 'What can I do to make sure that, when such a crisis occurs again, it is less disruptive?' It may be a long hard road, but this is the route to salvation.

There is no doubt which of these is the high-leverage activity, but we have no time to deal with it because the next crisis is already knocking at the door.

In some jobs, particularly in industries such as construction and publishing, the atmosphere of crisis seems endemic: organization is so poor that life becomes a series of crises. Those managers who plan can never stick to their plans, most managers have given up even trying to plan and, to them, my suggestions above seem ridiculous and idealistic. I know from personal experience that reacting to urgencies is a treadmill which leaves no time for planning. But I also know from personal experience that unless you plan, you will live on that treadmill for ever (unless it goes out of business). The route to salvation is to discover the underlying causes of the problems and solve them properly. It may be a long hard road, but there is gold at the end of it.

TRAP TWO: FIRE FIGHTING IS FUN

If we are honest with ourselves, we do like a minor crisis: two phones ringing; people in and out of the office; the adrenalin pumping away; the thrill of action; and time passing in a flash. That is good fun and it makes us feel important.

Fire prevention, on the other hand, may mean going back to the office, shutting the door and thinking – and that can be boring.

So we are tempted into fire fighting at the slightest opportunity, while the high-leverage fire prevention tasks sit on the desk waiting for tomorrow.

Society also glamorizes fire fighting. Films and TV programmes are full of it. Take Batman and Robin, for example: they rush round

Fire fighting is fun

week after week getting the baddies locked up in prison, but when did you last see them ask why there is so much crime in Gotham City? When did they ever discuss what should be done to improve the education system?

TRAP THREE: THE POST-ADRENALIN DIP

See if you recognize this scenario. You have just had a really good crisis, three hours of furious activity and excitement, but now at last the fire is out, the phones have stopped ringing, you get back to your desk and . . . nothing happens. You sit there pushing bits of paper about but achieve very little.

There is a physiological dimension to this problem. That burst of adrenalin we get in a crisis is part of our fight/flight response. It is the same burst our primitive ancestors on the plains of East Africa received when they were threatened by wild animals. The moment that danger is perceived, the body steps up its production of hormones which cause the heart to beat faster and more forcefully, increasing alertness. Blood pressure is increased and the blood flow is diverted from less immediately essential systems like digestion toward the muscles to give extra strength, and chemical changes occur in the blood so that it will clot more easily if we get wounded.

Today, all this happens to us when we get an awkward phone call from a customer. It is quite inappropriate!

The body, having been pumped up for action, later has to re-

Fire prevention is boring

balance itself, and there is a corresponding dip in our energy levels.

After a morning of teaching I find it very hard to do any productive work in the early afternoon. The best answer I have found is to simulate the fighting or running away by taking some physical exercise. A 15-minute walk, or even better, a swim, is an excellent way of relieving stress and tension, whether during the day or at the end. It is not as easy as taking a drink, but it is probably much better for you.

TRAP FOUR: FIRE FIGHTERS GET PROMOTED

In some organizations I have worked with, the ability to deal with crises is regarded as a prime qualification for promotion.

Imagine the scene. The new department head, whose entire reputation has been earned by fire fighting, hurries into the office one morning and finds . . . there are no fires to fight! So what does the fire fighter do? That's right, start some. 'Come on, let's have some more action round here! There aren't enough balls in the air.'

Such people work best in an atmosphere of crisis – and find ways of perpetuating it. They belong to the heroic school of management, always charging into battle. They can become addicted to their own adrenalin, unable to achieve much without a tight deadline. As a result, they come to love deadlines and pressure, and those tasks that don't have deadlines don't get done. Such people learn through experience on the job. They have neither time nor energy for other forms of learning or development. They don't read books.

Anyone who has a boss like that has my sympathy.

Other budding fire fighters achieve a similar result by a slightly more subtle route – they leave everything until the last minute. Anything can become a crisis if you leave it long enough. 'I work best to deadlines,' they say.

The problem with both these types is that they don't just create a crisis for themselves. It sucks in everyone around them, including the administrative and secretarial staff who usually don't like crises and don't work well in that environment.

In some organizations the problem becomes endemic, with everyone perpetually in crisis mode. On the odd occasion when the pressure does ease, people are far too tired to tackle high leverage tasks. They spend their time catching up with the filing, or just chatting together.

TRAP FIVE: COMFORTABLE, FAMILIAR, EASY TASKS

I don't think I have ever met a Finance Director who doesn't spend 15 minutes a day adding up numbers or checking the adding up of numbers. Suppose our Finance Director loses a debate at a board meeting and that someone is mildly rude to her, she comes out feeling rather low.

She goes back to her desk, pulls out some papers and a calculator and spends the next 15 minutes checking numbers. This is something she is very good at. It rebuilds her self-confidence and her ego. It helps her face the rest of the day.

We all have our hobbies and comfort zones into which we can retreat. What do you do at about 2.30p.m. when you are feeling a bit low and there is no immediate crisis? And did you remember to put it on your list of time-wasters?

Many managers decide at this time to 'walk the job'. They call it 'Managing By Wandering Around'. They think of it as a high-leverage task, motivating the staff. I am all for wandering around and motivating the staff, but what they are really doing, if the truth were told, is taking a break and interrupting everyone else.

We all need a break occasionally, and we might well need comfort zones to retreat into when we feel a bit battered. The important thing is that we realize what we are doing and restrict it to a reasonable timescale.

The worst instances of this trap of familiar and easy jobs are the managers who spend time doing the jobs they did before their last promotion. That is always a job they are familiar with and good at. Managers who do this are ruining two jobs simultaneously: they are failing to do their own jobs and are frustrating their successors.

TRAP SIX: IMMEDIATE REWARD

Many of us are suckers for immediate reward. We like the illusion of progress that comes from ticking things off on a list. If you start the day with 20 jobs to be done, it is nice to have ticked off ten by coffee break. But there is only one policy that will achieve this, and that is 'Always start with the little jobs' – which, of course, is the road to stagnation because the high-leverage activities are usually longer jobs and so get left for tomorrow.

Some people become addicted to ticking things off, and are always rushing round with a list in their hands. If you peep over their shoulder you will often find items like 'have lunch' on the list. Such a list allows them to tick off more things and feel that they are moving even faster. Quantity is always easier than quality.

Before we look at the answers to the problem of prioritizing, I suggest we have uncovered several more time-wasters which were missing from the original list. I am going to add them to the master list and, if you winced at any of them, I suggest you add them to your own list:

TIME-WASTERS

Travel
Social chat
LACK OF SKILL OR KNOWLEDGE
CREATING CRISES
LEAVING THINGS UNTIL THE LAST MINUTE

FIRE FIGHTING IS FUN
NEGLECT OF FIRE PREVENTION
POST-ADRENALIN DIP
COMFORTABLE, FAMILIAR EASY JOBS
IMMEDIATE REWARD

PRIORITIZING – THE ANSWER

As with most aspects of time management, the answer is very simple. There are three parts to it: how to identify your high-leverage tasks; how to devote more time to high-leverage tasks; and how to get the other tasks done faster.

Identifying your high-leverage tasks
Take some time to reflect on what would be high-leverage for you. What could you do in the next month that would make you more effective in the future, and set yourself some clear objectives.

Giving more time to high-leverage tasks
The answer to this lies in a profound little saying: 'More than two priorities is no priorities'. You cannot have ten priorities. If you think you have ten priorities, then you haven't got any priorities.

Something that has helped me enormously in recent years, is to head for work each day with one single priority – of course, you may have meetings, appointments and a reminder list with 20 items on it, but that is not a list of priorities and must not be confused with it. Start the day with one *high-leverage* activity as the single priority, your 'Task of the Day', and fight hard to make sure that, whatever else crops up, whatever crises occur, you make some significant progress on that task that day.

Using this approach, I find I have made better use of my time than I would have done otherwise.

Getting low-leverage tasks done faster
I don't need to tell you how to do that. You know the answer. Cast your mind back to your last major holiday. What happened in your office the day before you left?

My word you were ruthless then! You whistled through the list, doing things, delegating, throwing things away at an amazing speed.

Why not work like that normally and clear more time for high-leverage tasks? When the pressure is really on, the true priorities become clear. When you are going on holiday; when the project reaches its deadline; when the conference convenes; then you know, suddenly, what has to be done and what can be ignored; then you find ways of speeding things up. The solution is to allocate significant amounts of time to the high–leverage activities and put pressure on the other tasks on a daily basis.

Late in the afternoon turn to the accumulated E-mails and paper on your desk; say to yourself: 'I am going home at 5.30 and that lot is going before I do.' Give it the same focus and energy you would if you were going on holiday the next day, and it's amazing what you can get through in just 20 minutes.

CONFLICTING PRIORITIES

There is always a conflict between 'production today', which is doing your job, and 'building capacity for the future', by which I mean the high leverage tasks. What should your balance be between these two? It won't be possible to achieve a balance each day, but taking the perspective of a week or a month, it must be possible. Do you get that balance right?

There is also a conflict between priorities dictated by others and priorities chosen by yourself. Most people do first what their boss has told them to do, then what their customers have asked for, then their colleagues, their own staff, and even complete strangers are catered for. If there is any time left, then they'll do what they want to do. Well, the high leverage tasks are your agenda, and they shouldn't come last on any list. Again it's a question of balance. Do you get the balance right?

For some there is a conflict between being a technical expert – engineer, accountant, salesperson etc. – and being a professional manager. People enjoy using their expertise, it's tangible and satisfying, they do it well. In contrast managing is ambiguous and difficult, and to start with they can't do it well, so there is a strong force dragging them back to their area of expertise which can prevent them becoming experts at managing.

TOP PERFORMERS

I have met a wide variety of managers from many levels in a wide range of organizations. If I had to select the single characteristic that best distinguishes between the outstandingly successful and the worthy average, it would be prioritizing.

Top performers are ruthless about their priorities: they are crystal clear about what they are and, somehow or other, they manage to give them a lot more time. The vast majority of worthy, average managers spend their time rushing around, coping, patching, solving the same problem over and over and just getting by.

If you lose sight of your priorities you cannot be effective. I believe this to be the number one key to effective time management, and thus make no apology for continuing to re-emphasize it. The following is a true story.

Charles Schwab, one-time President of Bethlehem Steel, was complaining to a consultant about his terrible time pressures and said: 'If you can show me any way of making better use of my time, I'll pay you any fee within reason.'

The consultant said: 'Time Management is easy. I'll do that now. Sit down and list on this piece of paper everything you want to do tomorrow. Just brainstorm them in any order. Now go through that list and work out which is the most important item – not the most urgent, the most important. Put that at the head of another sheet, then find the next most important and so on. Rewrite the list in order of importance.

'Tomorrow, when you get to your office, start work on the job at the top of the list and work at it until you have finished it. Then go to the second and so on. If, at the end of the day, you have not got to the bottom of the list, don't worry. You couldn't have done better. Last task of the day – produce the list for the following day and prioritize it.'

A month later the consultant received a letter from Charles Schwab. He wrote to say 'Thank you, that is the best advice I have ever received', and enclosed a cheque for $20,000.

Now I am not expecting you to send me $20,000 as a result of reading this chapter, and I do know that you can't control your own time to that extent (nor can a Company President) but the moral is clear – if you take your eye off your priorities you can never be effective.

LESSONS FOR LIFE

Life as a whole has many opportunities for building capacity for the future. We can fill our days with routine activities and pleasures, or we can recognize that there is a future to be created. If you spend all your time caught up in the matters of today you will be condemned to do that tomorrow. If you can make some time for high leverage tasks, there is a chance that life will be easier or more pleasant in the future.

Take as an example the relationship between parents and children in the home. Every time the parents shout at the children and get them to tidy their rooms that is production today, but it doesn't do much for the relationship. Time spent playing with children, listening to them and working on their agenda is time spent building the relationship and increasing our ability to help them in the future.

The tragedy in some families is that all the time is spent getting the bedroom tidy, cooking, cleaning, and gardening and none goes into the relationship. When the children reach their teenage years and the identity crisis that these years bring, the relationship isn't strong enough to help them through, and by then it's too late to do anything about it.

Do you get the balance right?

SUMMARY

The French cavalry is reputed to have had a motto in the last century: 'If in doubt, gallop!' I can't help feeling that it has been adopted by many managers in this century. Busy, busy, busy all day long, but at the end of the day, what have you done? It is easy to be busy, any fool can be busy, but surely you are not paid to be busy – you are paid to be effective, and being effective means doing the right things. If you are not doing the right things it doesn't matter how hard you work.

That latter-day American philosopher Ziggy Ziggler puts it well:

> The Main Thing
> is to keep the Main Thing
> the Main Thing
> at all times

That is exactly what I am saying. Look again at your high-leverage list. Ask yourself 'What am I here for?' Write down your high-leverage tasks on a card and put it on your desk where it is always visible to remind yourself that 'This is what I'm here for'. Of course you have lots of other things to do – but this is where you can really make a difference in the long run.

3. *Procrastination*

Procrastination is an impressive word, but a debilitating disease. It is the practice of putting things off, developed by some into an art form.

When you have a difficult project to undertake, or an unpleasant task to perform, do you find it can take several days to make a start? Every time it comes to the top of the pile you think of something else that you must do first. Even otherwise unpleasant tasks like tidying the desk suddenly become attractive and urgent as a means of avoiding it. Some of us can be enormously creative in thinking up reasons to put off that unpleasant job, others just drift into daydreams.

Half-way through that boring job you might catch yourself scanning desperately for excuses, positively willing passers-by to come into your office. Even an irrelevant phone call can be seen as a blessing.

The problem has been around for a very long time. The word procrastination is derived from the Latin *procrastinatus*: to put back to tomorrow, to make it a matter for tomorrow. The well-known saying 'Procrastination is the thief of time' was written over 250 years ago by Edward Young, and it is as true today as it ever was. Procrastination steals your time, it prevents you from achieving, it puts pressure on tomorrow and it leads to stress, to deteriorating relationships and, ultimately, to loss of self-respect.

Clearly procrastination is not confined to the work environment. It can just as easily stop us decorating the spare room, tidying the garden or reading this book. Worst of all, it becomes a habit and a way of life. We develop little rituals at the start of the day: reading the newspaper, tidying the desk, rearranging the piles of paper, drinking coffee and having a chat with colleagues.

Procrastination is a form of incompetence. How would you feel if your computer took half an hour to warm up? How would you feel if the shop assistant took half an hour to get in the mood before he would serve you? How would you feel if you saw yourself taking half an hour to start work after reaching your desk in the morning?

I need two cups of coffee
before my brain gets going

Most people who read this book are likely to be motivated by achievement. We feel better when we get things done. That is really what this book is about – getting things done or, to be more precise, getting the right things done.

In order to accomplish anything it is necessary both to start it and to finish it, and procrastination can attack us at both ends. Poor starters wait for pressures to build and deadlines to loom: 'I work better under pressure'. They tend to live in an atmosphere of crisis and stress, which they inflict on colleagues and, by cutting things fine, they are always vulnerable to unexpected problems. Poor finishers tend to be enthusiastic, ambitious and over-committed. They have shelves of unread books and particular problems in controlling their desks. They get irritated by fussy people who are concerned with unimportant details – like finishing things.

The specific reasons for procrastination are many and varied, but here is a selection with some suggestions for killing this ubiquitous time-waster.

THE TASK IS TOO BIG, I DON'T KNOW WHERE TO START

Take time to plan the work on a major project, breaking it down into manageable units. The thought of walking 100 miles would be quite overwhelming, but we could all walk to the end of the road. In this way the formidable challenge of writing a report might become:

- Plan the structure of the report
- Gather all necessary information
- Write a first draft
- Refine and finish the report

None of these sub-tasks is quite as formidable as the overall task. Since we all recognize the power of deadlines, set yourself a deadline for each sub-task. This will also help to defeat Murphy's Law No. 5: 'Whatever needs to be done first can't be done without doing something else before it' which has sabotaged many a good intention

IT INVOLVES A DIFFICULT DECISION, I DON'T KNOW WHAT TO DO

- Assess the importance and urgency of the decision. Our culture seems to admire those who are decisive, and for unimportant decisions that may be the right approach. Make unimportant decisions fast so that perfection doesn't stand in the way of progress. On the other hand, if the decision is important, a poor decision made quickly could be disastrous. Start by deciding when the decision should be made.
- Collect any information you may need to make the decision and consult people who might be able to help. Recognize that you will never have *all* the information.
- List all the options you have, including the unlikely ones, then draw up separate lists of the advantages and disadvantages of each. Don't just run through them in your head, write them down.
- During the rest of the time until you need to make your decision try not to worry about it. Don't keep making and

remaking the decision. Devote yourself, instead, to the exploration and research. Try to think of other options. Try to find more advantages and disadvantages, always being careful to write them down. Challenge any assumptions you might have made.

- When the appointed time arrives, sit down and make the decision.
- Then, if it is a major decision, sleep on it before finally committing yourself. That will give the subconscious a chance to contribute. You may well wake up knowing the answer.
- Having committed yourself, consider the matter closed. Don't continue to worry about it.

IT INVOLVES DOING SOMETHING UNPLEASANT

The task may include confronting someone, asking a favour or taking a risk.

- Stop and analyse exactly what it is that you don't like about it. Should you set yourself the objective of resolving this underlying problem once and for all by signing up for a course in assertiveness, public speaking, or whatever the problem is?
- Draw up as a balance sheet the advantages and disadvantages of postponing action. This usually looks somewhat one-sided.

Advantages of postponement	Disadvantages
I might feel more like it later	It will hang over me
I could tidy my desk now	The problem can only get worse
I must see Mary as soon as she arrives	I will run out of time later
	I will feel stressed
	It will not help my self-image
	It will put pressure on my colleagues

I FEEL RATHER LOW AND DON'T HAVE THE ENERGY

Roger Black, in his book *Getting Things Done*, has an excellent suggestion for this situation. He calls it the BANJO method of management. BANJO stands for:

> Bang
> A
> Nasty
> Job
> Off

When you are feeling a bit low, maybe at 2.30pm, or for some people first thing in the morning, glance down your list of jobs to be done; select the most unpleasant one, the one you are least looking forward to – and do it immediately.

I would not suggest planning the whole day like this, but I find that the task in question is usually a five-minute job – an awkward phone call or letter – and that the psychological lift which results from having completed the worst job is most energizing. It makes the rest of the day seem easy.

I HAVE TROUBLE GETTING STARTED IN THE MORNING / AFTERNOON

- Discipline yourself to start doing real work within minutes of reaching your desk. Set this as a performance standard for yourself: 'I will always start work on a planned task within two minutes of reaching my desk'. If the task is complex and you don't know where to start, start anywhere. A bit of action will soon get the brain in gear and most tasks seem easier once they are under way.
- Cut off all obvious escape routes. One of the easiest ways to escape from a boring task is to see something much easier that needs to be done urgently. That is one reason why cluttered desks lead to inefficiency. Clear your desk, close the door and avoid sitting where you can see out of the window or see other people.
- Whenever you suspect an imminent attack of procrastination, set yourself some immediate targets. Make it a game.

I SUSPECT THAT I AM A POOR FINISHER

- Once again break down major tasks into sub-tasks. Discipline yourself to complete each task before moving on.

- Try to avoid feeling happy with progress, tell yourself that the work is of little value until it is finished.
- Find ways of rewarding yourself when you do finish a task or a sub-task: a cup of coffee, five minutes with the newspaper, a chat with a colleague, whatever turns you on!

AFTER EACH ATTACK OF PROCRASTINATION

Ask yourself why you succumbed. Why was it hard to get into the task? What escape route did I use? What can I do to avoid this next time?

TIME-WASTERS

Comfortable, familiar, easy jobs
Immediate reward
PROCRASTINATION

4. Personal Organization

About one third of the managers I meet seem to have some problem of disorganization, one of the symptoms of which tends to be an untidy desk (possibly in parallel with cluttered computer files and a cluttered home). Some of these desks are quite spectacular, disappearing under piles of paper! Difficult and boring jobs accumulate, along with unread reports, half-completed tasks and last month's journals. Sometimes they bear a sign saying 'A cluttered desk is a sign of genius'.

If you put yourself into this genius category I ask you to remember the times you have spent searching desperately through the piles for something that has become critical, and the occasional embarrassment of failing to find it and turning up at the meeting without the relevant papers or agenda.

I invite you to remember the other occasions when, not under quite so much pressure, you have sifted gently through the piles to see if anything was about to become critical. And, above all, I ask you to remember that terrible disease, the spring-cleaning bug. From time to time you suffer a bad attack of spring-cleaning. You get into work extra early, you roll up your sleeves and you spread out the paper all over the desk, and the floor too. You put like with like, you file some, you throw some away and the remainder is put in neat piles on the desk. By lunch-time you feel pleased with yourself – you can actually see the surface of the desk and you think you have done a really good morning's work.

You haven't done any work at all. You have just been shuffling paper. That doesn't produce anything, sell anything or motivate your people. It certainly isn't high-leverage. In fact it is not even work, it's a complete waste of time and must be added to the list of time-wasters. Tidying the desk without changing the systems achieves nothing because the disorganized piles reappear within days (and you didn't need me to tell you that).

This drama is enacted daily in thousands of offices. If it is happening to someone else it is a comedy. If it is happening to you it is a tragedy.

As before, the superficial answer is simple: focus on your 'goods inward' procedure.

HANDLING INCOMING PAPER

When a piece of paper, or the electronic equivalent, lands on your desk you have three options:

- First ask yourself 'Am I ever going to do anything with this?' Unless you are absolutely certain that the answer is yes, throw it away now! If it's important it will come back again. Now you might think that is a bit dangerous, but have you ever noticed, when you go through the spring-cleaning ritual at your desk, how much paper you throw away without reading it? And much of the paper you don't throw away you only keep because it isn't old enough yet – it will get thrown out next time. What rubbish! Why not throw it away as soon as it arrives and save all that bother? And that junk in the back of your garage, are you really going to use it again?
- If the answer to 'Am I ever going to do anything with this?' is 'Yes, definitely', then the second question is 'Can I do it now?'

It is the original time-management principle, and a very sound one – do it now. There need be no conflict between this and prioritizing. If it's a five-minute job or less do it immediately. It's much more efficient for the organization, much more helpful for your colleagues and, above all, it saves you having to remember it, keep it on the desk, shuffle it around and write it on lists! Do it now. It would be wrong to schedule the whole day like this, but every time you clear your In-tray and E-mails (twice a day?) simple tasks should be done immediately and fast, if possible hand-writing replies on the original documents.

- 'Can I do it now?' If the answer is 'No', then the final action is to file it. But we don't, do we? We put it on a pile on the desk. And that is where the real problems start.

A HISTORY OF CLUTTERED DESKS

I became interested in time management because I was bad at it. The more I taught the subject, the better I became at it, except in this one area. I knew that I had been able to help other people organize themselves and clear up their own cluttered desks, but I couldn't do it myself. One day a member of a course, who had been totally taken in by the brilliance of what I had said, subsequently caught sight of my office and was so horrified that he borrowed a polaroid camera, took a photograph of the desk and circulated it round the group. I thought that was a bit below the belt, but it did make me think again. How could I teach the subject when I couldn't practise it?

I re-read everything I could find on the subject of personal organization, desperately searching for help, but found it all quite useless. I suddenly realized that most of it had been written by people who were highly organized, who didn't face the same problems that I faced. I decided that this was a golden opportunity. I, as a sufferer, must find my own answer, so that I could help fellow sufferers.

As I knew the problem to be very prevalent among the sort of people who teach in business schools, I circulated a note to all my colleagues announcing that I was forming a support group for people with a chronic untidy-desk problem. The response was fascinating. Notes like that are normally ignored, but on this occasion no fewer than seven people took the trouble to reply and all of them said the same thing: 'What a good idea, I wholeheartedly support your initiative – please tell me what the outcome is, but I'm too busy to come to your meeting'. This demonstrated another symptom of disorganization: organized people can always find the time for something that is interesting, disorganized people are under too much pressure.

One person announced that he would come to the meeting – and then forgot about it. That's another symptom. Another colleague, who is by repute the most disorganized of all, didn't turn up. I caught him in the corridor a few days later and said 'Owen, why didn't you come?' He said 'It's not a problem'. 'Owen, that's not what I hear,' I said. 'No', he said, 'I've solved it!' 'Tell me more', I said. 'Well', said Owen, 'every time I receive a document which I think might be important, I get my secretary to take a copy of it, so if I can't find it, she can give me hers.' I fear that's not an answer.

The ultimate prize went to another colleague who approached me two months later, brandishing my note and said 'I've just found this, I wish I'd known!'

The support group did meet, and spent an hour discussing personal organization. We made a most interesting discovery. Each of us, no matter how untidy our desks, could identify some area of our lives in which we were well-organized. For me, it was my finances. I know what I've got in the bank, I have a cash-flow projection for the next 12 months and I know what I owe the tax man. It's all thoroughly organized in detail. Several of my colleagues were amazed at that. How had I done it? Well, many years ago I set up a system which is easy to keep up to date.

Another colleague said that he had a collection of CDs, records and tapes, all immaculately labelled and organized, and kept in a special cabinet. I found that quite amazing. I've got some CDs and tapes all jumbled up in the corner. I can never find anything. His collection is his pride and joy – he's devoted time to setting up a system. That is the first part of the answer. Those who are disorganized have to invest time in setting up systems.

THE POWER OF SYSTEMS

The system for causing quality is prevention. Devote time to setting up systems to eliminate error and inefficiency forever. Build in feedback loops so that you will regularly evaluate and improve your systems. Think of the benefits good systems can bring: greater productivity, more certainty, improved self-image, improved morale, more respect from colleagues and reduced stress.

DISCOVERING THE REAL PROBLEMS

If you are serious about organizing your desk, then start by doing some research. Go and sit at your desk one day when it's in a particular mess (right now maybe?). Do not tidy it, that's the last thing you should do, just sit there. Take a clip board or pad and analyse the situation. Work your way across the desk and ask of every single thing that is sitting on your desk: Why is that sitting there? Why did I put that there? Why have I not filed that?

Force yourself to write down your answers to these questions. Some of the answers will occur again and again. What will emerge will be a series of problems, each of which needs to be solved.

Tidying the desk may seem simple, but *organizing* the desk – setting up the systems that will allow you to keep it tidy – presents a series of problems, and is therefore much more complex. Most people fail to solve these problems because they devote all their energy to tidying the desk and none to organizing it.

WHY DO YOU PUT THINGS ON YOUR DESK?

When I ask people that question, one of the most common answers is 'Because I haven't read it yet'. Many of us have a deep psychological feeling that files are for things which have been finished with. It took me many years to discover that files can be used for things I haven't read.

Another common answer is 'If I file it, I will forget it' – out of sight is out of mind. This may be true. The trouble is that when you're struggling with that difficult report your eyes wander across to the pending file, and you think 'Oh! I'll just do that now.'

Get it out of sight – but in order to ensure that you don't forget it, you need a reliable system of lists. Write the item on a list and file the document. Use the list to trigger the action and not the document. At some point you have to make the big psychological step from being *document-driven* to being *list-driven*. At this point you will discover a fascinating difference between piles and lists. While a

Environmental pollution

document placed on a pile will naturally gravitate towards the bottom, an item written on a list will automatically rise towards the top.

Another common excuse is 'There isn't a file with the right name on.' Maybe half an hour spent thinking about your filing system, setting up some new files – bring-forward files, meeting files, etc. – could help.

When I applied this research technique to myself, I found myself saying 'I haven't filed that because I haven't finished it.' When I found 12 things on my desk which I hadn't finished, some of which hadn't been finished for six months, and clearly no longer needed finishing but starting again, it became apparent to me that I had a chronic problem of *not finishing things*.

So, do the research. When you have identified your own list of problems don't try and solve them all simultaneously – that would be asking too much. Choose one problem which seems to occur quite frequently, set up a system to ensure that nothing ever sits on your desk again for that reason, and concentrate on sticking to the system for a few days. Next time the desk looks bad, or next time you can generate the energy to do something about it, do the research again, select another problem and design a system to solve it. Gradually, over a period of weeks, you will get organized and it will become easier and easier to keep your desk under control.

The next step is to set clear standards for the job. One of these might be 'Clear the desk each day before going home.' If it's done every day it will never be more than ten minutes work; if you leave it for a couple of weeks, it can be an impossible job.

Incidentally, sweeping everything into a pile in the cupboard does not count as desk-clearing.

IS IT A CHRONIC PROBLEM?

For acute sufferers, I suggest the 'Antiques Roadshow' test. As you sit at your desk tomorrow, examine all the paper on it and, purely as a matter of academic interest, try to work out which piece of paper has been sitting on your desk the longest – one month, three months, six months, twelve months? You might find some real period pieces. When you've found the oldest one, ask yourself 'how important was it?' It usually wasn't.

The simple advice peddled in many books, 'Handle each piece of paper only once', led me to devise another sadistic exercise for acute sufferers: find out how often you handle each piece of paper. Put a sharp pencil on the right hand side of the desk, and every time you touch a piece of paper, make a mark on it on the top left hand corner. When it arrives in your in-tray and you pick it up to see what it is, mark it. Later, when you put it in your briefcase, mark it. When you pull it out at home, mark it. The next morning, if you take it out of your briefcase, mark it. Then, if you move it to look for something underneath it, mark it. When you find 20 marks on the same piece of paper, stand up and scream as loud as you can: there must be a better way.

Finally, for the really chronic sufferers, you must separate the task of setting up systems from the task of digging yourself out from the backlog. My suggestion is to get a second desk (most chronic sufferers already have two, and sometimes even three desks), put all the backlog on the other desks and try and run your main desk to the new system. Only when you've set up systems that enable you to keep it clear do you start digging out from the backlog. It took me 12 months.

Sir John Harvey-Jones put it rather well: 'I don't like clutter. At a minimum it may say that the executive is disorganized; it may say something about lack of clarity and it may say he or she is not coping with the job'. Something frequently said by those with a cluttered desk is 'A clear desk is a sign of a sick mind.' I sometimes think that might be true, but the untidy desk does cause stress, waste of time and loss of face with colleagues – and the illness is curable.

If you *must* keep several things on your desk, make sure they are your most important, high-leverage projects – not the rubbish.

FILING SYSTEMS

Most people file far too much. Research shows that 80 per cent of the documents filed in offices are never looked at again. Don't run a 'Just in case' system. Ask yourself, when considering whether to file, 'If I threw it out and then found I needed it, what would be the consequences?' Excessive record-keeping is often a sign of insecurity.

On the other hand, if it *is* worth keeping then it is probably worth knowing how to find it again. It's a good idea to create a plan of your filing system to aid recovery. A good filing system has relatively few headings, though the files themselves may be quite thick. A bad system has one hundred and fifty files, many with one piece of paper in. Paperclips are a nuisance in files: they catch other documents, or fall off. Staples are better.

One useful device which has helped me is to have a 'decay pile'. Any incoming document which I don't think I will need, but about which I am not quite certain goes on top of the decay pile. Every month I throw away the bottom half of this pile. I never look through to see what is in it (though occasionally I can retrieve something from it when it has become relevant). It is like having a wastepaper basket that is only emptied monthly.

COMPUTERS AND OTHER TECHNOLOGY

Computers frequently appear on the list of time-wasters. For some this means waiting for access, or being thrown off by those with higher priority; for others it can be an afternoon spent exploring the esoteric elements in the graphing package (hobbies, on our list); and for others the problem is that computers do not understand simple instructions. We get stuck in cul-de-sacs from which there is no escape. We press 'help' and it doesn't; 'cancel', 'escape' and 'log off' suddenly mean nothing to it. (In desperation I have even tried some other 'offs', but it remains unmoved). The real problem is, of course, *lack of training*.

Telephones have become much more sophisticated in recent years. Do you use the call back, call forward, conference call and other options? Some executives struggle to transfer a call. Voicemail is a service to your clients and colleagues, especially where you have nobody to take your calls when you are away.

E-mails and faxes are fast, flexible and cheap, and can often be used in place of a meeting. They have another great benefit: unlike the telephone, they don't interrupt.

Small portable tape recorders are handy for capturing ideas.

A small alarm clock on my desk is always set to buzz five minutes before my next appointment. This helps me to be ready, and frees my mind to concentrate right up to that deadline.

INADEQUATE SUPPORT

Some organizations try to save money by purchasing cheap equipment, others by reducing the numbers of support staff. In both cases this can result in highly-paid executives spending time and energy on mundane jobs like photocopying.

FIRST IMPRESSIONS

If I were to enter your office, what is the first impression I would form from looking around? Effective and efficient? Or chaotic and messy? First impressions *matter*. Walk through your building one quiet day. Look into each of the offices and assess the character of the owner from the general appearance of the room. Then do the same for your own.

Does your work area have:

- A place for everything and everything in its place?
- A substantial clear area in which to work?
- Telephone and natural light to the left of the desks for right-handed managers?
- Something personal to give it character?

Time-wasters

You will have noticed that, at the end of each chapter I am extracting any new time-wasters that have turned up and adding them to my master list. I trust that you are taking any which are familiar to you and adding them to your own list. There are five candidates for this chapter:

Immediate reward
Procrastination
CLUTTERED DESK
SPRING-CLEANING THE DESK
POOR FILING SYSTEM
LACK OF RELIABLE LISTS
NOT FINISHING THINGS

5. Interruptions

'LIFE IS A SERIES OF INTERRUPTIONS'

I am sitting at my desk trying to write a report. I have been at it for half an hour. The framework is now clear, the words are beginning to flow and I have written the first four paragraphs when I hear that dreaded knock at the door. It's Eddie.

"Have you got a moment?"

Suppose I manage to deal with Eddie's query in just five minutes. How much time will it cost me in the production of that report? Ten minutes? Fifteen minutes?

It is worse than that. Ten minutes ago the internal post arrived, and with great presence of mind I managed to persuade myself that I should ignore it because I was writing the report. But, now that I have been distracted, I had better have a look and see if there is anything urgent, and there is (there always is when you want there to be). So I deal with it. Then I remember the phone call I meant to make earlier and I make that. By that time I am feeling so distracted I think I could do with a cup of coffee to settle me down. In the kitchen I meet Ian and we stop and chat for ten minutes. One way and another I do not get back to that report today. How much time has it cost me?

Now I am not suggesting that you ban all interruptions, because a large part of your job is being available to colleagues and others. In Victorian days, managers were people who hid behind closed doors with secretaries guarding the way and nobody could get in without an appointment: I would not wish to go back to that for a moment. But these days we have gone too far in the other direction. 'Open-door management' has become a virility symbol: the door must be open at all times. How often are the problems that walk in through your open door high-leverage tasks?

In any job there are some tasks that need a high level of concentration. When I ask managers how they handle such high-concentration tasks, the answers usually include the following:

- 'I hide in the training room, where there is no phone'
- 'I come in early, before anyone else is here'
- 'I stay late'
- 'I take them home'

In fact, the general consensus tends to be that you can't do any work in the office between nine and five. That has to be wrong.

Every manager must have a barrier to keep out interruptions, ideally a permeable barrier which will let through the real crisis but keep out the trivia.

Personal secretaries were ideal for this, but anyone can close the door and divert the phone. It is legitimate to do this for meetings and interviews: it must be legitimate to do it when you are tackling a task which requires a high level of concentration. Whenever you close the door you must also bar the telephone. If you don't have a secretary or voicemail, do a deal with a colleague: 'you answer my phone for half an hour today and I will do the same for you some other day.'

If none of these is possible, then the answer may be to do the work at home – not at nine o'clock in the evening, but by going home early, or coming in late.

In recent years, when London Underground was on strike and some commuters were taking three or four hours to travel to work, a few enlightened employers told people not to struggle into the office but to stay at home: 'Take some work with you and do what you can from home'. They found that a lot of people did much more work at home than they did in the office. Some jobs – and people – might benefit from having work restructured to allow one or two days a week working from home.

Open-plan offices

Increasingly, people are working in environments without a door, in open-plan offices. There are advantages in open-plan: it does allow a team to communicate during the day, and if properly laid out with plenty of space, sound baffles and the insulation of noisy equipment, it can work well. If, on the other hand, the purpose of open-plan has been that of the prison – containment at minimum cost, an excuse to cram more people in per square foot than could possibly be done with partitions – the effect is usually disastrous on both effectiveness and morale.

Is your work area large enough? Is it quiet enough? Is it acceptably private? Can you divert your phone?

How many managers have done a cost benefit analysis on open-plan offices? What is the saving achieved by cramming more people into the same office? What is the effect on their performance?

The environments in which we ask some people to work are appalling. If I was working in an open-plan office I would go out and buy some ear muffs, not little discreet ones, great big fluffy ones: Mickey Mouse ears to wear when I needed to concentrate, just to show people when I did not want to know.

In order to be made workable an open-plan office must have meeting rooms, where people can hide when they need to concentrate, and adequate staff to answer the telephones of those who are away from their desks. For those who are working in open-plan environments I suggest an occasional meeting of all occupants to identify the principal problems and discuss ideas for improving the environment.

Open plan offices can work – I have seen some good ones – and some organizations are now experimenting with different designs of office space: quiet cubicles with PCs for individual work; round tables and coffee machines for informal get-togethers; and secure rooms for formal meetings and interviews.

Signalling systems

One of my favourite stories is of a senior software engineer in an open-plan environment at Hewlett Packard. He was being destroyed by interruptions. One day, in desperation, he went out and bought the largest teddy bear he could find. He sat it on the filing cabinet beside his desk and sent a note round to everyone in the department: 'When the teddy bear is sitting smiling at you, please feel free to come and talk to me. When it is standing on its head facing the wall, I do not want to know, even if the building is burning down'. For the next two days there were endless jokes about this man and his teddy bear, but everybody recognized it as a serious attempt to tackle a genuine problem. After a few days he could get virtual total privacy, at least from the trivia, simply by turning his teddy bear round.

The lesson of this story is important. What we need is a visible signal that says 'I do not want to know'. The signal can be very simple, such as sitting at the opposite side of the desk with your back to the door. This can be particularly effective where there is a glass panel in the door. It means that you won't see people waving and pulling faces at you. It makes it harder for them to interrupt.

Some managers have a sign on the door saying, 'DO NOT DISTURB', which is a bit crude. Others have a sign that says 'MEETING IN PROGRESS'. I don't like that when it's not true. In some parts of BT managers have a traffic-light system, red, amber and green.

Whatever your system is, you must then train people to respect it. When someone does break through your barrier – comes in when the door is closed, ignores your teddy bear, or whatever – it is important that you let them know, politely, that they have trans-gressed. Be ruthless with the time, but be kind to the people. Get up and meet them in the doorway, don't let them make it to the chair. Greet them warmly, and when they have said what they want, explain your situation. Tell them that you will deal with it later or will call them back as soon as you have finished the report or whatever you are concentrating on. If you allow them to achieve their purpose they will do the same again tomorrow.

A woman rang me recently and said, 'It works! It works!'

'What works?' I said nervously.

'Your interruption idea. I put a sign on my PC saying "Report writing in progress, please come back after 11.00a.m!" One of the directors came out and stood right next to me. I kept my head down. He stood there for a minute. My concentration was blown, but I kept tapping the keys. Then he said to someone across the room, "It looks as though Jane is busy. I don't think she wants to talk to me," and he went away – it works!' That is what most of us fail to do: we don't train people to respect our privacy.

If the same people are interrupting you regularly, you might consider setting up a daily meeting or phone call at a set time. If Karen knows that I will see her at four o'clock each day, most things will wait until then. If possible, arrange such meetings in the other person's office. That way you control their length.

ADVICE FOR ALL

Whatever your strategy for protecting yourself from interruptions – and I emphasize that you must have one – there are several tips which may help it to work better:

- Do not abuse your strategy. I have no patience with the person whose door is closed for seven hours a day and open for one. They are solving their own problems at the expense of incon-veniencing everyone else. We should be available to our customers, colleagues, boss and others as much of the time as possible – indeed successful senior managers often spend a large part of their days in informal meetings – but it is OK to put up the barriers occasionally.

- If I want to get hold of you and your barriers are up, I would like to find out from your voicemail or whoever is answering your phone when you will be available. I would also like to be able to leave a message, confident that you will receive it and act on it promptly. Some of the people I deal with are very good at this and I respect their privacy. The secretaries of others never know where they are or when they will be back. Their voice-mails say they are away from their desk but don't tell you whether they've nipped out for a coffee or gone to Brazil. If I leave a message it disappears into a black hole. Under those circumstances I shall batter away until I get through the barrier. Many of those who complain about interruptions are their own worst enemies. They are not fair with other people.
- Another aid to concentration is the pre-emptive strike. Immediately before doing the high-concentration tasks, walk the job and pick up any simmering problems. That will often give you a clearer start.
- In some jobs it is possible to have a regular time for high-concentration tasks. You might manage to train your colleagues to leave you alone between 10 and 12 for example.

PERSONAL FAILINGS

Interruptions are among the most visible and irritating of time-wasters. They are always one of the first things to be mentioned on any list and they are, indeed, very costly, not only in terms of time, but also in motivation and creativity. Most people have experienced that sense of deep involvement, a feeling of gentle euphoria, that comes with total immersion in some problem, unaware of passing time.

But how often do you achieve that? It seems to take 10–15 minutes to reach that level of involvement, yet research suggests that most managers are interrupted once every ten minutes! What will the quality of your work be if it is written in 12 separate periods of ten minutes each with crises in between, as compared with one straight hour of concentration? And what does it do to your motivation and commitment to be interrupted every time you get interested? Where serious thought is needed it is important to concentrate on one thing at a time.

The term we use to describe this problem – 'Interruptions' – immediately points the finger of blame at the interrupters but, as in all sections of this book, we must also ask, in what ways do we contribute to this problem ourselves?

Could it be that high-concentration tasks sometimes get a bit lonely? That we sometimes hope for an interruption? When Eddie came into my office at the start of this chapter, he came to ask my advice and that is nice. I like that, it makes me feel important. I strongly suspect that many of us are ambivalent about interruptions: we complain about them; we use them as an excuse for our failure to complete high-leverage tasks, yet we do very little to discourage them. In fact at another level interruptions can be quite welcome.

Have you ever noticed how you get more interruption-prone when you are doing a really boring job?

I am sitting in my office, writing; the words are not flowing very well and the brain is aching; I hear footsteps in the corridor; I recognize them; I look up and nod at Eddie, positively willing him to drop in; and then I call it an interruption. I suggest that some of us should add to our list of time-wasters:

TIME-WASTERS

Lack of reliable lists
Not finishing things
ENJOYING INTERRUPTIONS
ALLOWING UNNECESSARY INTERRUPTIONS
OPEN-PLAN OFFICES

In every job there are certain tasks that require concentration. You must find some way of giving them that concentration.

6. Reading

The volume of reading matter received by managers seems to increase every year, especially for more senior managers. Reading always appears on the list of time-wasters.

WHAT SHOULD YOU READ?

Most managers seem to spend between one and three hours a day reading. Much of this time is spent reading things to see whether they need to read them, and when they get to the end the answer is often 'No. I didn't need to read it.'

Consider this scenario. You get back to your desk after a two-week holiday or business trip and find a large pile of paper waiting for you. You sort it into two piles: urgent and interesting things in one pile; and the rest in the other. Over the next few days you deal with the urgent and interesting items and other new items which come in, but the boring pile sits and looks at you. Some people take it home at night for a change of scenery, but either way it doesn't get read. Eventually, after a couple of weeks (for some people a couple of months) you realize that you are never going to read it, you put it in the waste paper basket and the world does not stop. So do you really need to read those things for the rest of the year?

It is mere common sense never to undertake a piece of work, or read a book, without asking 'Is it worth the amount of life it will cost?'

I suspect that reading is one of those nice easy tasks that we can do when we are feeling low, when we have a few spare minutes, or while watching TV. It becomes a hobby and we never stop to analyse its worth. How much time do you spend reading work-related material in a typical day? Even one hour per day, five days per week, 47 weeks per year is a significant slice of your life. It could easily amount to ten per cent of the entire time you spend working. Do you get full value from the time you spend reading?

Taking the pending file home for a change of scenery

Reading can be delegated or shared. In some offices, large numbers of people glance at the same journals and circulars. Why not share these out so that each journal is read early and thoroughly by one person on behalf of the whole department? That person would be responsible for bringing anything important to the attention of everyone else.

Analyse your normal reading material and throw out as much as you dare. There may well be other reading matter that you could get more value from, like some good management books, but stop reading things just because they land on your desk. Make your own decisions about what to read.

HOW GOOD ARE YOU AT READING?

Most of the managers I work with are not very skilful readers. They learned to read at school and then ignored this vital skill.

Reading, like any skill, can be developed. With training and practice anyone can read better and there are many courses on effective reading, but only about one manager in 12 has tried them. A high proportion of those who have taken such a course report that it helped them – some say it helped enormously.

Many years ago I bought a book on effective reading. I spent about 30 minutes a night working on it, two or three nights a week, for about two months. By the end of that time I had doubled my reading speed and more than doubled my effectiveness.

How are your reading skills? Do you know how they compare with others'? Would you like to find out?

The passage below is a reading test. This five-minute speed-reading test was created by Hilda Yoder, of the Yoder School, New York City. Originally appearing in Carl Heyel's *Organising, Your Job in Management*, the 500-word selection is of standard difficulty, the kind of material found in newspapers and general magazines. Time yourself as you read it, then consult the graph that follows to calculate your reading speed. Read it at your normal reading speed for light material. It is not a technical passage or a legal contract, so read it as you would read an article in your daily newspaper.

Anyone can read quickly – if they don't bother to understand – so I warn you that there are some questions at the end to check your comprehension, but don't let that put you off.

READING TEST

Note your starting time:
Chances are good that you are stuffing your briefcase with more and more material to read at home. In virtually all middle- and top-level jobs, the flood of 'required reading' has steadily increased.

Yet more businessmen could cut drastically – or even eliminate – the amount of such work they take home. The secret: developing more efficient reading habits.

Statistics show that most businessmen read below the college level – attaining only 300 words a minute or less – and that their comprehension of the material is far too low, and that 90 per cent of them could at least double their reading speed and – much more important – boost their comprehension considerably.

To a slow reader, increasing speed and comprehension may seem impossible.

He is likely to feel that the ability to read fast is a God-given talent possessed by only a favoured few.

Actually, the rapid reader has received no such mystic blessing. The way a person reads is nothing more than a habit. And the slow, poor reader, by study and application, can usually become a good reader.

One way to change your reading habits is to go to a good clinic or teacher for a special course. This may well double or even triple the average executive's reading speed. One reason for this is the fact that methods for analysing reading faults have been developed on a highly scientific plan. Here is just one example. The actual movements of your eye can be photographed, giving a graphic picture of such things as the number of fixations per line of type, backtracking, length of time to read a specific number of words.

But can you improve your reading skill on your own, without going to a professional source? Yes – if you are willing to study and practise. Just reading a book about how to improve your reading won't work, any more than just reading about exercise will strengthen your muscles.

Here are the broad principles involved. Authorities have found that most businessmen are likely to be perfectionists in reading. They read every word because they are afraid of missing something. Reading whole thoughts and phrases increases both speed and comprehension.

The best way to do this is by reading material of standard difficulty, such as most popular magazines or light novels. Time yourself, see how much you read in, say, ten minutes. Next day read the same length of time but try to read more text.

While doing this, concentrate on moving forward. Don't regress, or look back, trying to pick up something you missed. You will have trouble getting the full meaning at first, but the important thing here is to jostle yourself out of old reading habits.

One way to test your comprehension is to have someone ask you questions on what you have just read. A better way is to do this is reading from books specifically designed to improve your skill. They include tests on comprehension that relate to their text.

Finishing Time:
Now calculate your reading speed from the graph below.

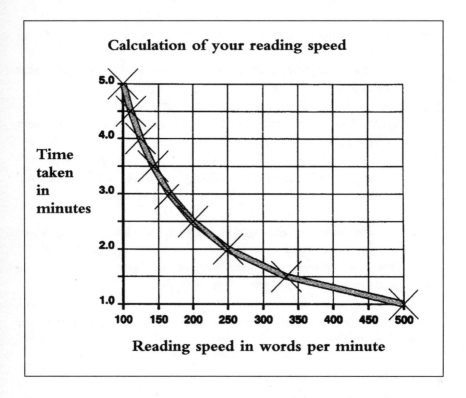

Calculation of your reading speed

Time taken in minutes

Reading speed in words per minute

A few of the managers taking this test read as slowly as 180 words per minute. Most read at between 200 and 250 words, with a significant number up to 320, and a few very much faster than that. The fastest are usually around 500 words per minute.

COMPREHENSION

To evaluate your comprehension of what you have just read, tick the answers to the following true/false questions about it.

1. To cut his homework, a businessman needs to develop better reading habits.
   T –   F –

2. 99 per cent of businessmen can improve their reading.
   T –   F –
3. Good reading is a matter of good habits.
   T –   F –
4. Reading habits can be analysed.
   T –   F –
5. Reading techniques can be improved merely by knowing your difficulties.
   T –   F –
6. Perfectionists who must note every detail tend to be poor readers.
   T –   F –
7. Reading can be improved by looking for whole thoughts and phrases.
   T –   F –
8. The best way to improve reading is to choose for daily practice a book you find difficult to read.
   T –   F –
9. Looking back for a missed idea is a 'must'.
   T –   F –
10. Comprehension can be developed by reading books written for this purpose.
    T –   F –

Score	Rating
6 or lower	Poor
7	Passing
8	Good
9	Very good
10	Excellent

PLANNING TO READ

Planning has arisen several times before as a key to the effective use of time, and planning before reading is another example. Before starting on any material ask yourself:

- What is my objective?
- What do I know already?
- What am I looking for?

This will help you to decide how to tackle it and how fast to read it. Different material should be read at different speeds. If you are reading a technical passage, or checking a document for detail, you may well have to read at about 150 words per minute and there is not much that an effective reading programme can do to help. However, I find that many people who do a lot of this detailed slow work read everything at the same laborious pace. Some material should be read very much faster and, if you know what you are looking for, large parts can be missed out altogether.

Skim-reading is a useful skill. By skimming at about 3,000 or more words per minute it is possible to understand just enough about a passage to know whether you need to read it.

PREVIEW ALL MATERIAL

When reading anything substantial, preview it. Glance through at the headings and illustrations, see if there is a summary, get an overview of the whole piece.

Tony Buzan, psychologist and best-selling author of *Use Your Head*, suggests that you treat a book like a jigsaw puzzle. With a puzzle you don't start at the top left of the picture and work along in linear fashion; you start with the most interesting feature, then move to the next most interesting, and so on, leaving the boring sea and sky until the end. So, too, with many books: start with the most interesting bits, then in-fill, and when it gets boring put it down.

Reading and writing are inefficient ways of transferring information. As an author, I take an holistic thought which I wish to make available to you, an unknown reader; I have to translate that thought into a linear stream of words, which is sometimes a painful process; then, several months or years later, you read that stream of words and construct an holistic thought. Oh, for the day when we learn to use telepathy!

CONCENTRATE

Many people fear that if they read faster they will understand less. Research shows that the opposite is true: on average those who regularly read quickly tend to understand better than those who read slowly.

This is not so surprising when we realize that our minds work so much faster than we can take in the printed word. When reading slowly, the mind gets bored, and goes away to do something else.

I used to try to read in the evenings. I would sit there with my eyes following the words, my fingers turning the pages and my brain doing something else. What a complete and utter waste of time! If you are going to do nothing, then do nothing properly. If you are going to read, then read properly. Reading needs concentration.

STOP BACK-SKIPPING

This is a common problem among slow readers, especially those who read at less than 200 words per minute. You think you have missed something so you go back and read it again. There are two main reasons for back-skipping. The first is that the concentration has lapsed. The second is a technical one: as you read, the image from the page strikes the eye almost immediately and the message is transmitted to the brain almost instantaneously; but then it sometimes takes the brain a second or two to digest this incoming information, log it in with other similar information and let you know that it has understood.

In that split second you think you have missed it, so you read it again. Don't do that. As long as your mind was on the job, keep going and you will usually find that you have understood it.

MOVE YOUR EYES FASTER

This is another of those ridiculously simple tips: if you want to read faster, then move your eyes faster. Like many simple answers, it is true. It seems to be very difficult to speed up gradually.

When you do move your eyes faster you will find that you cannot read properly. Don't worry: with practice, you will find that you start to see more and more of the words and, eventually, you will learn to read accurately at that faster speed.

EYE MOVEMENTS

Human beings cannot see when their eyes are in motion; you only see when your eyes are stationary. You can test that: swing your eyes slowly round the room. You will see a series of still pictures; it is very rapid, but each is a separate still picture. So, when you read a printed passage, you look at the first word, then jerk your eyes to the next, and the next, and so on, in a series of rapid fixations. Speeding up your reading therefore means shortening the time taken for each fixation, and sometimes using fewer fixations.

One useful gimmick to help push the eyes along faster is not to look at the first or last word on any line. When you focus your eyes on an object you are aware of anything close to the object. Try it. Focus your eyes on the middle word in this phase:

Read more books

and you can see the whole phrase. Make use of this peripheral vision to reduce the number of fixations you make in a single line. Start reading each line by focusing on the second word – you will see the first word – and when you get to the next to last word, move on to the next line – you will see the last word.

Slow readers also make many irregular eye movements. It is fascinating to observe them. Take a page of print, make a hole in the centre with a hole punch, then ask someone to read it silently as you watch their eye movements through the hole.

DEVELOPING YOUR SKILL

There are many good courses on reading skills, but you can never develop a skill on a short course – it needs practice.

My suggestion is to buy a book on reading skills. The one I used was *Read Better, Read Faster*, by Manya and Eric de Leeuw (Penguin) but there are many others. Much of the content of these books is a series of passages for practice – ignore these and practise on the low-grade reading that you do each day, such as newspapers.

Read the first chapter in a reading skills book, then practise whatever skill or habit is being recommended for the next week or two whenever you are reading anything unimportant. Then go back to the book and find the next technique. This way you improve your reading skills with very little investment of time. But be warned – it is hard work.

SUMMARY

- Assess the value of your regular reading and cut out some low-value items. Undisciplined reading of junk mail and low-value material is a terrible time-waster
- Plan your reading, setting clear objectives before plunging in
- Develop your reading skills so that you can read some material much faster
- Learn to read different material at different speeds

I am often asked whether speed-reading takes the fun out of leisure reading – which is a bit like suggesting that learning to drive might take the pleasure out of walking. I choose to do much of my leisure reading quite quickly, but if I am particularly enjoying something, especially if it is well-written in elegant prose, I will frequently slow down to about 240 words a minute and savour it.

TIME-WASTERS

Enjoying interruptions
Allowing unnecessary interruptions
READING LOW-VALUE MATERIAL
POOR READING SKILLS
LACK OF CONCENTRATION

7. Memory

What happens to the information after you've read it or heard it? How long do you remember it? I would like you to estimate the efficiency of your memory.

Throughout the day our senses are bombarded by thousands of stimuli. We are constantly seeing, hearing, feeling and smelling our environment. We deal with this vast array of information by ignoring most of it and focusing our attention on a few elements.

Complete the graph below by drawing a line to show how fast you think you forget things. Start your line with only those stimuli that have actually got into your mind; the things you have seen, heard or felt at any given time. Presumably you will have forgotten some of them at some point in the future. When? How fast? Is it a

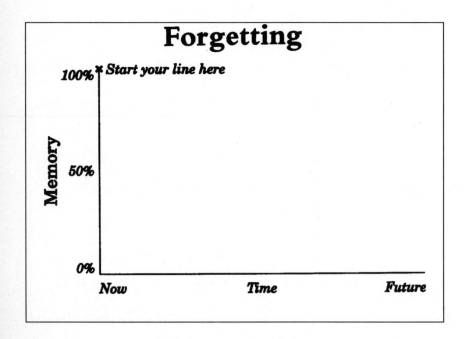

straight line or a curved line? Please put in your own timescale along the bottom: you can measure in days, weeks, months or minutes, whichever you think is most appropriate. In particular, how long do you think it takes for you to forget 50 per cent of what you have taken in? Difficult, I know. You will say it depends on how interesting the information is and how it's presented to you – but broadly, as an average, have a go.

Most people grossly overestimate their capacity to remember, perhaps because we know what we remember but rarely notice what we have forgotten. The results of scientific research into the way we remember and forget are shown on the graph below.

Most of the stimuli we take in are unimportant to us, and so we forget them within an hour or two. If that seems surprising to you, then reflect for a moment: Did you read a newspaper this morning? How many of the articles you looked at can you now remember, unprompted? You would be doing well to remember 20 per cent.

You may notice that on my graph of forgetting the line starts by going up. I believe that for complex inputs, the brain takes time to digest and integrate them, and that shortly after we have read or heard something we may understand it better than we did at the

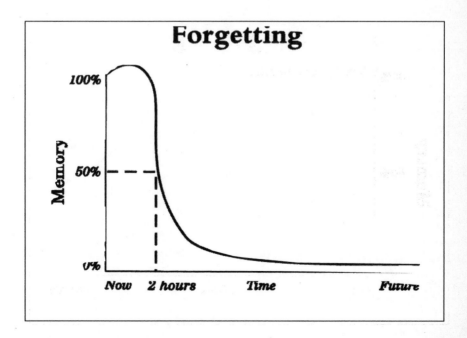

61

time. But quite soon, the rot sets in. Most of the information we receive we do not need to remember and it disappears from unprompted memory very quickly. Those items which are interesting or important are much more likely to be remembered. However, we sometimes forget things we would have preferred to remember.

While tidying out a file some months ago I found some very interesting information. It was quite new to me, yet was definitely written in my handwriting. The item was some notes I had made after reading a book about five years earlier. I had probably forgotten them within two weeks, and now there was no trace left in my memory. What a waste of effort and time! What can we do about that?

The answer, which I adopted several years ago and which has been very helpful to me, involves setting up a learning system. Whenever I attend a seminar, read a book, or in some other way find something I want to remember, I take a few minutes at the end to summarize the key points – no lengthy notes, just a few key words; pictures are even better. The next day I glance at these notes and they do serve as keys: they unlock and refresh a lot more detail about the material. I glance at these key words every day for two or three days,

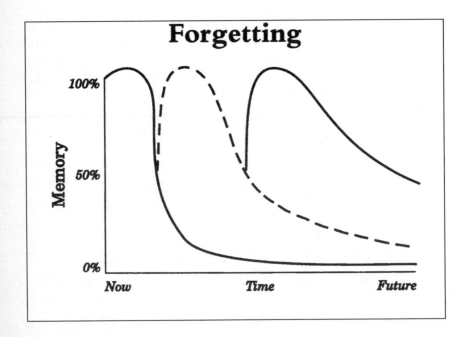

by which time there is a much greater chance that the information will have got into my long-term memory.

The best way to do this is on 'mind maps', a technique devised by Tony Buzan, using pictures, colour and as few words as possible to capture ideas.

I suspect that most managers have forgotten many useful tips and pieces of information which could have been valuable to them, and thus 'forgetting' enters the list of time-wasters – or rather 'failure to learn and remember'.

TIME-WASTERS

Poor reading skills
Lack of concentration
FORGETTING
FAILURE TO LEARN AND REMEMBER

This also applies to remembering names. Some people seem to be able to do this naturally, others, among whom I was one, gaily say they can't remember names.

I discovered that I would often not know somebody's name within two minutes of being introduced, which gave me no chance the next day. I also discovered that if I make sure I hear a name and put a little effort into learning it, my memory for names improves dramatically. If I take 30 minutes on the first day of a management course I can learn the names of the 36 participants without much difficulty. So could you, with a little practice.

8. Working Hours

How many hours do you work in a typical week? I suggest you include in this sum all the time you spend at your place of work from arrival to departure, whatever you are doing, including lunch and coffee breaks. Add to that any time you spend on work-related matters in the evenings and at weekends. Do not include commuting time, unless you are reading on a train. If you travel a lot in your job, allow some of that, but take out the equivalent of commuting.

What does it come to? fifty hours? sixty hours? Even more?

Do you ever feel tired at work? If the answer is 'No', then move on to the next chapter, but if, like ordinary mortals, your answer is 'Yes', then please pause again for a moment and reflect on what happens to your performance when you are tired.

When I feel tired:

. . . .
. . . .
. . . .

Here are some of the common answers I get to that question. When I feel tired, I:

- Work more slowly, things take longer
- Make more mistakes
- Become less creative and tend to rely on stock answers
- Listen less and become more autocratic
- Get irritable and take it out on someone

Does this sound like the super-effective executive you would like to be? Long hours and consequent tiredness can be one of the main causes of poor use of time. In some offices people boast about their long hours. Some even boast about how little time they have for their families. For such places there is a slogan, which should be prominently displayed:

FATIGUE IS NOT A BATTLE HONOUR
IT IS A CRIME

Surely, managers should be fit for the job – physically fit, which means having time for exercise and proper eating; and mentally fit, which means leading a balanced life.

Many people drift into a pattern of long hours without ever seriously thinking about it. Parkinson's Law, when applied to time, states that 'Work expands to fill the time available', and it is absolutely right. If you have decided not to leave the office until 7 o'clock, there will always be work to keep you there until 7. If you have decided to take a briefcase home each night, there will always be work to put in that briefcase. If you have decided to pop in on Saturdays for a couple of hours, there will always be work to do on Saturdays. In fact, if you were an insomniac workaholic and you allocated 140 hours a week to work, the job would soon expand to fill 140 hours. And you still wouldn't have finished – because you can't finish.

The good news is that if work expands to fill the time available, the opposite must also be true: work must be able to contract to liberate the time that should not have been available. Having spent many years working excessive hours myself and having more recently talked to many others who have fallen into that trap, I think I have discovered the answer. Each of us should decide 'What is a reasonable length of working week for me?' and fit the work to the time, *not* the other way round.

There will always be the occasional crisis week when you have to work 60 or 70 hours – that is part of the price you pay for the magnificent salary you draw – but if you normally work a 65 hour week, what will you do when the crisis arrives?

Similarly it may well be right to work a 65 hour week when you take on a new job, to spend extra time understanding the new role, setting up systems, building new relationships etc., but only for a limited period.

Many of the people who work long hours think that they have to stay at work until they have 'finished'. Well, you can't 'finish', I hope we've established this. But if they think they are going to finish they see little need to plan and prioritize, which makes them ineffective. On the other hand anyone who is going to work a 45 hour week, especially when those around them work 55 hours, will have to plan and prioritize and as a result might be more effective.

I have had people come to me because they are working too many hours at considerable cost to their health and family life. My advice to them is to cut their hours, immediately, to 45 or whatever they consider reasonable. Again and again they come back later and tell me they are achieving more in 45 hours than they were in 65. 'I'm in control of my job now, it's not driving me.'

Several months after attending a two-week management programme, Fiona commented that 'At the time I felt I was not being pushed hard enough, there was not enough pressure, but I now recognize that it has changed my life. I have cut down my hours: I am delegating far more and have become a better manager, but most important of all, I think it has saved my marriage.'

Some organizations have a culture of long hours: it is not done to be seen leaving at the official finishing time; people say things like 'Have a nice holiday' or 'Working a half day today?' as you walk out; there is great competition to be first in or last to leave; and people believe that long hours show dedication, which is what leads to promotion.

Surely any sensible organization will ultimately judge on performance, not hours. If you are achieving the results, you must ignore the jibes and stop feeling guilty about going home on time. Organizations that reward long hours are penalizing the effective people, and senior managers who work long hours are creating a very poor role model. In one such organization I know, where they have a six-month panic every year and expect everyone to put in excessive hours, I have asked some of the younger staff how they keep it up, how they manage to work until 7 or 8 each night: 'Well, I pace myself. I take a two-hour lunch break. I read a novel in the afternoon.' All so that they can be seen to be there at 7 o'clock in the evening. What nonsense!

We turn at the end of this chapter to personal failings, to the underlying psychological reasons why people fall into the trap of long hours. I have identified three major ones: laziness, poor sense of time and the inability to say 'no'.

LAZINESS

Inside many workaholics there is a lazy child, filling the day with comfortable, easy, familiar tasks, but hiding their laziness from themselves and others behind a smoke screen of long hours. Nobody who is working a 70-hour week could possibly be called lazy: they try to prove to themselves that they are dedicated and hard working, but fail to recognize any possibilities for change.

POOR SENSE OF TIME

Some people seem to assume that time is unlimited. They expect to work until they have finished. If you believe that you can finish, and if you expect to stay at your desk until you have finished, there is no need to plan and prioritize because everything will get done. Such people disappear into work, the weeks get longer and longer and they are far too busy to notice that they don't always finish, and that all too often it is the high-leverage tasks that are left for next week, next month – and eventually for the next person who does their job.

INABILITY TO SAY 'NO'

Still others like to be kind and helpful. They do everything that is asked of them, whether it is part of their job or not. They tend to get put upon and fill their time with low-leverage jobs that should really be done by someone else. You will find further advice on the use of the word 'No' in chapter 11.

All these reasons stem from a confusion of *activity* with *results*. Workaholics become addicted to activity and spend their time complaining in aggrieved tones that they don't have enough time and that they are overworked. To them, and to any other workaholics that you may know, I dedicate the cartoon on the next page.

The key to effective management is *leverage*, not longer hours. To put it in the words of my wife when I used to open my briefcase in the evening, after a twelve-hour day in the office: 'You must be awfully inefficient if you can't get it done in twelve hours.'

The most painful thing was that she was right.

So what is a reasonable working week? There is no single answer: it depends on the nature of your work, the amount of variety in your

'Mummy, why does
Daddy bring home
so much work?'

'Because he doesn't
have time to do it
in the office dear'

'Then why don't they
put him in the
slower group?'

working day and, above all, on the balance you wish to achieve in your life. Some chief executives work an enormous number of hours. They have chosen to dedicate their lives to their work, to the virtual exclusion of family and other interests. Fine: they have the right to make that choice – as long as they realize that it is a choice, it is not compulsory. They have no right to impose it on others

At the other extreme, W V Publications, a small magazine publisher in Camden, tells its staff that the office hours are 9.30 to 5.30 (this in an industry renowned for its long hours); that the office is unlocked at 9 and locked again at 6; that they should not take work home and that they are encouraged to take a lunch break; but that when they are in the office they are expected to work hard.

What a good idea!

TIME-WASTERS

Forgetting
Failure to learn and remember
WORKING LONG HOURS
BEING TIRED
LAZINESS
POOR SENSE OF TIME
INABILITY TO SAY 'NO'

9. Travel

For many managers, travel appears high on the list of time-wasters.

For the past 200 years, the speed at which man has been able to travel has increased steadily – yet the average amount of time people spend travelling has increased in parallel. We choose to live further from our work, further from the shops and further from our parents. Many of us choose to live where there is little public transport and spend time running a taxi service for our children. When we do get a break from this daily grind of travel, we spend our holidays . . . travelling!

TRAVEL AS A SOURCE OF STRESS

Driving is one of the major causes of stress. Even driving at a steady speed on clear roads demands concentration and alertness; driving in a hurry on crowded roads is far worse.

Air and rail travel are also stressful. No matter how experienced the traveller, and how apparently relaxed, all travel is tiring, even without the all-too-frequent delays.

TRAVEL AS AN OPPORTUNITY

On the other hand, most managers make little effort to reduce the time they spend travelling, so they must be gaining some benefit from it. I suspect that, for many busy people, the time they spend travelling is almost the only time they get to themselves, free from interruptions, to think and to reflect; to digest and integrate the affairs of the day, and to plan for the next few hours. In this context, mobile phones can become a major problem. They enable people to hurl messages at you whenever they want, targeted like smart bombs to deprive you of your peace. It may be nice to feel wanted and important, but do you really need that reassurance all the time?

I am all for mobile phones, but only for outgoing calls. Don't give anyone the number.

Certainly, I find air travel an excellent opportunity to read and to plan. On a one-day visit to de Baak in the Netherlands I can usually read a management book, as well as do a full day's work. Carrying reading material on such journeys also means that any delay to the schedules immediately becomes an opportunity – to read more.

Mobile phone – message targeted like a smart bomb

TRAVELLING TO WORK

Whatever the potential opportunities presented by travel, it is still a time-waster. It is at its worst where it is hardest to spot – probably in the habitual daily commuting run.

Since my commuting run now amounts to ten minutes per day, compared with at least 90 minutes per day previously, I am saving 80 minutes every day. That means 6½ hours per week, or 300 hours per year of prime working time.

In other words, after seven years in my present job, I had saved over 2,000 hours. That is roughly the number of hours we work in a year. Now that is worth having! A whole year saved – and I have been able to choose how to spend it.

If commuting can't be avoided, what about travelling early to avoid the traffic? Many executives are good at doing this in the mornings, but what about the end of the day? If you regularly get to work early, discipline yourself to leave at 4.30p.m. twice a week.

BUSINESS TRAVEL

Do you really have to visit them? Are you sure a ten-minute phone call and/or a fax couldn't achieve the same purpose? And if you must meet, why not invite them to visit you? It is all too easy to commit yourself to long hours of travel without due thought – though sometimes it is valuable to see others in their own environment.

The stresses of travel can be minimized by using checklists: one for packing, so that you never leave anything behind; and one for the journey, listing everything you must do, all journey times and any telephone numbers and other information you may need. This latter list helps to free the mind to do real work during the journey.

10. Meetings

There is only one thing worse than going to meetings . . . and that is not being invited.

In the UK it is estimated that 4 million hours per day are spent in meetings. If nine people sit down to a meeting from 2.00p.m. to 4.30p.m., that meeting costs three working days. Meetings are so expensive in terms of management time and yet so important for effective performance that they deserve a book to themselves (and they have got one: *Effective Meetings* by Philip and Jane Hodgson). But meetings cause so much frustration and irritation that a brief chapter on them is necessary here.

In most lists of time-wasters, 'meetings' will appear among the top three or four items. I always ask the list writers to specify whether the meetings they have in mind are meetings they themselves have called, or whether they are meetings called by someone else. Almost invariably it is other people's meetings that they have in mind. It is interesting that the people who call the meetings never come on my courses.

Now that cannot be true. Other people's meetings will usually seem much worse to you. Indeed, one group of managers who do not often put meetings high on their list of time-wasters is Chief Executives – because they chair most of the meetings they attend. But if you find other people's meetings a problem, it is a fair bet that your people will be putting your meetings on their list of time-wasters.

At the end of a particularly grisly two-hour meeting of a sales team, one of the old hands turned to a new recruit and said 'Don't worry. Not all sales meetings are a waste of time. Some of them are cancelled.' Could your people be saying that?

The worst aspect of ineffective meetings is not just the colossal waste of management time, but the message they send to everyone that time is not important. When planning or agreeing to attend a meeting, ask yourself the following two questions:

- Is it necessary?
  We do need some meetings, but they are so expensive that we should always explore alternative methods of achieving our objectives. For example, meetings are a very inefficient medium for one-way passing of information: people can read far faster than they can speak; they can read at their desks, at a time that suits them; and when they are reading they can skip the boring bits. Think twice before holding a meeting. Don't hold a £500 meeting to tackle a £200 problem.
- Is everyone needed for the whole meeting?
  In my early days in newspapers, my boss held a Friday meeting, attended by all 18 managers in the department. It wasn't really a meeting, more an ego trip for the boss. It started at 9.30a.m. and wandered on until about 12.30. My active participation usually amounted to less than half an hour, so I sat there, bored out of my mind, for two and half hours every week. I can still picture that office. There was a large clock on one wall, with a full-size second hand. It was the slowest clock I ever watched. One day I made a fascinating discovery. I found that my metabolism got so slow during the meeting that I could hold my breath for two minutes. I was really proud of that! Normally, one minute would be the maximum. I started experimenting and got my pulse rate down to 48 . . . There is more to life than that. Don't imprison your colleagues. If someone is only needed for one item, put it first on the agenda then let them leave.

Here are some suggestions for more effective meetings:

- There must be an agenda.
  This should be circulated in advance, so that people can plan their contributions and bring all necessary information. Most useful are those which list both topic and purpose: Are we going to take a decision? Are we going to generate ideas? Or are we just going to chat about it?
- Papers must be circulated in advance.
  It is useful to have a clear performance standard, such as 'All

reports and papers must be in the hands of everyone who is coming to the meeting 24 hours before the meeting', combined with a second one: 'All circulated papers will be read before coming to the meeting.'

- People must prepare.
  Ten minutes preparation will often save ten minutes in the meeting, but the preparation will usually be by one person and the meeting may involve six. Preparation is particularly important for the person who will chair the meeting.

- Chairperson.
  I believe that the most important role for the person in the chair is to manage the process of the meeting: to keep the discussion focused on the agenda; to watch the clock; to ensure that decisions are taken; to shut up the over-talkative and bring in the quieter people; in general, to act as a sort of referee. I also believe that you cannot be both referee and centre forward at the same time. You may think it works, but others know it doesn't: problems frequently occur when the person who is

supposed to be in the chair becomes a protagonist in a debate, and suddenly nobody is acting as referee.

There is no reason why the most senior person present must take the chair. In fact, for departmental meetings, there are many advantages in having a rotating chair. If Kath chairs the meeting this month and Anthony next month, the results will be different. If we then discuss these differences we will all learn something about the skills of chairing meetings. A good referee is usually to be found close to the action. Likewise it is easier to chair a meeting from the centre of the group, not from the end of a long table.

To anyone who asks advice on how to chair a meeting, I would say: introduce each topic, referee the discussion, summarize at the end, and don't hesitate to blow the whistle for foul play and full time.

- Start and finish times.
Sometimes it is seen as a sign of status to arrive late. In one company I worked with I suggested that they had an unwritten objective: nobody would ever go to a meeting until everyone else was already there. The situation was laughable. If a six-person meeting starts just five minutes late, that is *half an hour of valuable time lost*. Meetings must start on time. If someone chooses to be late, that's their problem. Start without them. If the chairman of the meeting arrives late I would still start without them. Likewise, many meetings (though not all meetings) should have a published finishing time and stick to it. It is a bit like clearing the desk before your holiday. If there is a deadline at 4.00p.m. a lot of minor items can be dealt with very rapidly in the last ten minutes which might otherwise have taken half an hour.
- Flip charts.
I find visual aids a great help in keeping a discussion focused. If we are discussing the advantages and disadvantages of a particular proposal we can list them for everyone to see. In a badly-run meeting, you can offer to act as the scribe: *you* then decide what to write up and what not to write up; *you* decide where to write it and how big to write it. Used with subtlety this can give you considerable influence over the meeting.
- Adjournments.
Personally, I do not like to sit still for more than an hour: parts

of my anatomy go to sleep including, sometimes, my brain. People need to get up and move around, and indeed a great deal of work can get done in the adjournments. Picture the scene at the management meeting: Bill suddenly thinks of something he wants to say to Valerie, but it is not quite on the subject under discussion; Alison doesn't understand something Bob says; all sorts of subsidiary agendas get built up. If we have an adjournment, all these issues can get dealt with and the meeting may well progress faster as a result. Now if an adjournment means that everyone rushes back to their desk to make phone calls, then it becomes counter-productive. Likewise, if the adjournment is too brief, all these productive discussions take place in the washrooms and the minority sex is disenfranchised. An adjournment should mean that the group moves from formal mode to informal mode.

During the meeting, there tends to be only one person talking at any one time (and an unknown number listening). As soon as the adjournment is called, three or four active conversations start up, mostly about the subject or process of the meeting, so it would be reasonable to guess that more work is done in the adjournments. Early in my career I was heavily involved in industrial relations, and I learned then that most significant movement occurs in the adjournments, not in the meetings. So maximise the adjournments and minimize the meetings.

- Minutes.

For most meetings all that is needed is a brief record of the decisions that were taken and the actions people agreed to. Recording the entire discussion is cumbersome and unnecessary.

The time to produce the minutes is immediately after the meeting. To produce the minutes of the monthly meeting 29 days later, the day before the next month's meeting, is bureaucratic stupidity.

Where it is necessary to have a more complete record, and where all parties must agree the minutes, as with site meetings in the construction industry, a lot of time and argument can be saved by writing the minutes visibly on a flip chart as the meeting progresses – best of all on an electronic flip chart that can produce copies on the spot.

When I am taking the minutes I note down the key points as the meeting progresses, leaving plenty of space. At the end of the meeting I stay in the meeting room and fill in the gaps – it never takes more than five minutes. If you leave that job until next week you will have a major task to recreate the minutes. If you even go back to your desk the phone will ring, someone will pounce and you will have made the job harder. Stay where you are and finish them at once.

You can have fun with this. If you can type the minutes into your E-mail system within five minutes you may well get them onto your colleagues' screens before they get back to their desks, and that can be quite scary for them. 'How did you do that? Did you write them before the meeting?'

- Are your meetings fun?

When you call a meeting, is there a sudden rush to the box office? Is everyone keen to get in? They ought to be! We are social beings, we enjoy the company of others, so meetings ought to be the highlight of the week. And they can be. The secret ingredient is 'feedback'. In the words of the *One Minute Manager*, 'Feedback is the breakfast of champions.' Without feedback we keep attending the same meeting and nothing improves.

I would bet that you could tell your boss how to improve his/her meetings . . . and that your people could tell you how to improve yours. But you have to ask.

At the next meeting of your team, put at the end of the agenda an item called 'Review of process' and ask your people for their suggestions. The first time you do this they may not believe you. The second time someone may test you with some silly or minor suggestion and everybody will watch you carefully to see if you really mean it. The next time you will start to get real feedback, and after a little while the meetings will improve dramatically. Everyone will get a feeling of ownership – it's part of the process of empowerment.

11. Stress and Health

Stress drains energy. It lowers resistance to illness by suppressing the immune system. It impairs our judgment and performance, makes us less happy and less self-confident and, ultimately, can lead to mental or physical illness, even to breakdown. That is a terrible waste of time. Research suggests that over 60 per cent of all absences from work are in some way stress-related.

It is important to distinguish between two elements in this problem. First, there are the external forces which impact on us, which I will call 'pressure'; secondly, there is the way we each react to these external forces, which I will call 'stress'. Thus the amount of stress you suffer will depend in part on the amount of pressure put upon you, and in part on your ability to cope with that pressure.

We all know people who fall ill very easily under the slightest pressure, and others who get up at six, hold breakfast meetings, do five jobs at once, never get home before nine if at all, work most of the weekend – and wouldn't have it any other way. Such people often say that they thrive on pressure – which could equally be called challenge, or stimulus – and they are right. The effect of pressure on performance can be plotted on what is called an 'arousal curve'.

At very low levels of external pressure, people feel bored, frustrated and uninvolved. Performance is likely to be low. As the amount of external pressure increases, people become interested, stimulated, alert and effective. The more stimulus they receive the better they feel . . . up to a point.

Beyond that invisible point their efficiency begins to deteriorate – they feel overloaded, have trouble concentrating, procrastination can become acute and they make mistakes, often taking rash decisions. Ultimately, if the external pressure gets even greater, and especially if it continues for an extended time, the individual becomes indecisive, anxious, obsessive and is likely to become physically ill, possibly to the point of breakdown.

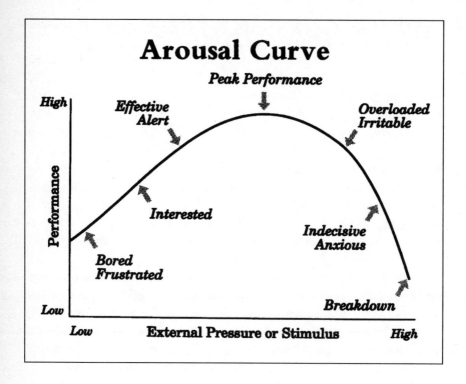

CAUSES OF STRESS

Any external pressure can cause stress, but some forms of pressure are particularly associated with high levels of stress. These pressures can stem from family life as well as work life and it is the accumulation of such pressures that causes the damage. Among the most common are:

- Major changes, such as moving house or job
- Entrances and exits from the family, i.e. birth, death, marriage, separation and divorce, or a breakdown in an important relationship
- Having responsibility without authority. It used to be thought that the most stressful jobs in business were the most senior ones – but senior managers *think* they're in control, and that's enough to reduce the stress. It's more often in the middle of an organization that we find people who feel responsible for something

without being in control of it, or who feel inadequate to undertake the responsibility
- Frustrated career plans, or any other major gaps in the mind between what should be and what is
- Frequent upsets to body rhythms, such as jet lag and shift work
- Tight deadlines and the need for prolonged concentration, as in driving
- Noise
- Doing things which you believe to be unethical
- Almost every item on our list of time-wasters. To that extent the whole book is about managing stress.

SYMPTOMS OF STRESS

Symptoms vary from person to person, but here are some of the most common, starting with the milder ones:

- Muscular tension in the lower back, shoulders and neck
- Disturbed sleep patterns
- Raised blood pressure
- Frequent headaches, indigestion and acid build-up in the stomach
- Inability to switch off and relax
- Difficulty in concentrating, thinking clearly, or remembering
- Loss of perspective, leading to obsessive behaviour. Those who smoke, smoke more. Those who drink, drink more. Those who work 70 hours a week, work 80 hours. This is often combined with excessive irritability and loss of temper
- Loss of interest in work and family, loss of self-confidence, dislike of self
- Ulcers, diabetes and asthma can be triggered by stress
- Continuing stress exhausts the body's systems and lowers resistance to disease. Many doctors reckon that over 50 per cent of health problems are related in some way to stress
- Physical or mental breakdown, heart attacks, even cancer

I made an interesting discovery about stress when I started running management courses. As a tutor, I try to get to know all 36 participants and to monitor and react to their needs over a four-week period. It's great fun; the adrenalin makes me feel alert and creative, which seems to be one of the best ways of avoiding illness – I have never even had a cold when tutoring a course. By the end of four weeks I am tired, but elated. Then the course disperses, the tiredness catches up, the adrenalin ebbs away and I might fall ill – not seriously, just catch a cold, or some minor bug. I have since noticed this happening to many other people after a period of particular pressure. Mind and body are very closely connected.

Some people seem to believe that the answer to this is not to stop but to keep going all the time. They have what is known as 'hurry up' sickness. If they are reading this book, they will be skimming, so I had better put some larger type to catch their attention:

- **ARE YOU AMBITIOUS AND COMPETITIVE?**
- **ARE YOU ACHIEVEMENT-ORIENTED AND DEMANDING?**
- **DO YOU SEE TIME PRESSURES AS POSITIVE?**

Such people are full of enthusiasm and drive; they push themselves and others relentlessly and they accomplish a lot. They like to be in charge, working hard and playing hard, always setting and beating targets whether they are in the office or playing squash.

Their enthusiasm and energy sometimes becomes aggression. Their high standards lead them to be overly critical of others. They behave as though their job is to give ulcers, not to have them. They are quick to blame other people for problems and are usually unaware that they are not good managers. They are certainly not good team members.

To such people I suggest that having a heart attack is not a sign of commitment, it is a waste of time.

RELIEF FROM STRESS

The following are commonly chosen to relieve stress:
- Alcohol
- Tranquilizers

These are particularly dangerous. By dealing with the symptoms they distract the sufferer from tackling the underlying causes. If you normally take two drinks to relax at the end of a hard day, an increase in stress is likely to make that three drinks, and you are on a dangerous route. It is difficult to analyse a problem objectively after drinking a bottle of wine, especially when you see yourself as a victim.

Much more effective relief can come from:

- Human companionship
- Physical exercise
- Relaxation techniques
- Healthy eating

Human companionship is an excellent relaxer, either in the form of a sympathetic ear or a good laugh. Indeed many people now believe that one of the main reasons why men suffer more stress-related illness than women is that they are, on average, much less good at giving and receiving this support. Maybe they can learn from the women around them. Unfortunately highly stressed people often need a few drinks before they can establish sufficient rapport.

Exercise is probably the best quick fix. It burns off the toxins that accumulate in the body when we are angry and frustrated – it is virtually impossible to worry and jog at the same time. The really enthusiastic hard-drivers can beat this one though – by jogging against the clock. For them, everything has to be competitive.

There are also many good relaxation techniques: physical relaxation, such as the Alexander Technique or progressive muscle relaxation; mental relaxation, creative visualization; and meditation. Anyone who leads a stressful life should study one or two of these so that they can be used to reduce stress and lower blood pressure, even in the midst of a hectic schedule.

Eating and stress seem to be related. Some people eat as a comfort when they are stressed, others lose interest in food and stop eating when stressed. Both can lead to problems.

REDUCING STRESS BY CHANGING YOUR MIND

- Logical analysis
- Positive thinking
- Problem solving

If you are feeling generally stressed, it is worth asking yourself: 'Where are the pressures coming from? What is causing me to feel stressed?'

This is particularly true for those who are inclined to wake at two o'clock in the morning and worry. The problem is that we are thinking only negative thoughts, we are not taking a balanced view.

Mental rehearsal is a natural and useful human habit, where we run through the situations we are likely to face and plan how to tackle them. Chronic worry is a perversion of this, in which we jump from problem to problem without thinking of solutions.

It is quite possible, even at 2.00a.m., to force yourself to think in a more balanced way. Ask yourself:

- What is the worst that could happen and can I cope with that?
- When did I last feel like this and what happened later?
- Will it matter in five years' time?
- Whose problem is it?
- What options do I have?

Another suggestion for the night-time worrier is to write down all your worries before going to bed – to make sure you don't forget them – then leave the piece of paper in your living room so that you can pick it up again in the morning.

REDUCING STRESS BY CHANGING YOUR BEHAVIOUR

- Time management
- Personal organization
- Assertiveness
- Goal setting

If time wasters are a source of pressure, then time management skills are a means of reducing stress. Hence the title of this book. If you take control of your time you reduce stress.

This applies particularly to personal organization. I've met people who sometimes play a game just before taking the children to school. It's called 'hunt the car keys'. Stress levels go through the roof. Other versions of this are played in offices daily. They can easily be eliminated by a little organization (see chapter 4).

The Magic Word 'No'

A common problem of poor time managers is over-commitment. It is also a frequent cause of stress. Therefore a key element in effective time management must be the word 'No'. It is a very simple word, but some people have an awful lot of trouble with it. Request: 'I'm a bit short of material for the house journal. Could you write me a piece on XYZ?' Response: 'Well, I'm awfully busy at the moment, I'm not sure whether I can find the time . . .'

What does that response mean? It could be translated as: 'Well, I'd like to help you, but I'm a bit disorganized at the moment and I don't know whether I can find the time. So please give me credit for wanting to help, and if you push me hard enough I will try, but I might not get it done in time, and if I fail it won't be my fault because I did warn you.' Well! Really! Does that sound efficient?

Most people want to be friendly and co-operative, yet some take the easy way out and allow others to trample on them. As a result, they become overloaded and exploited. They may be outwardly passive, but inside they are seething. Eventually the pressures and resentments build to the point where they explode in anger, leading to humiliation and resentment. Those who avoid the explosion and keep the resentment bottled up fall ill.

Far better to recognize that you have the right to say 'No'. It can be said politely and pleasantly but firmly. Not 'I don't know', 'I'll think about it' or 'Maybe', but 'No'. It means standing up for your own rights and saying what you want in an open, honest way, giving and receiving feedback.

When someone agrees to do something for me, I assume they are committing themselves to do the job properly and on time. I would far rather they said 'No' than take the task away and fail to deliver.

The root of the problem lies in low self-esteem and lack of self-confidence, but assertiveness also demands certain communication skills which can be learned. It involves describing your own feelings and views using 'I' statements: 'I don't think that's my job', 'I am starting to get angry'. It means controlling your voice and body language: where the aggressive person will stare and shout with a strident voice and a pointing finger, and the passive, non-assertive person will avoid eye contact and speak quietly and hesitantly while shifting positions, the assertive communicator will appear relaxed and in control. Above all it means maintaining a logical and unemotional approach to the situation.

There are some excellent short courses on assertiveness and many participants find them invaluable. Assertiveness builds self-confidence and the ability to stand up for your own rights – which must be good for time management.

Lack of clear goals is another cause of stress – either because you have nothing to do, as in unemployment, or because you have far too much to do, as in employment. Clear goals are motivating and energizing and thus help to reduce stress (see chapter 23).

Long-term health

If ill health is seen as a time-waster, then the prevention of ill health is a high-leverage activity. Better still, focus on the promotion and development of good health. Take advice on diet, health and exercise and increase your available energy.

Sleep is particularly important to our ability to tolerate pressure. Many busy executives find that, with practice, they can manage with only 6 or 7 hours sleep a night. Fine – one hour saved per night is the equivalent of 45 extra eight hour days per year – but do recognize that you will need more sleep at times of stress or illness.

12. Time Logs

Have you ever recorded what you do throughout a working day? Do you know how you spend your working time? How much time do you spend on the phone? How often are you interrupted? How much discretionary time do you have, when you can decide what to work on? How much time do you spend on your top priorities?

Few people can answer these questions accurately. Many managers are very surprised when they calculate their real use of time. Time is a scarce resource which should be budgeted, but how can you budget your time accurately when you don't know how you are spending it now; when you don't know how long each task takes?

Some time-wasters are highly visible, intensely irritating and cost us ten minutes a week. Others, often pleasanter jobs, cost us many hours a week but are rarely listed as time-wasters. The first step in improving any system is to get accurate information on the existing performance. Analysing the way you actually spend your time through a time log can often help to identify the real problems.

Draw up a sheet on which to log your use of time, such as the one shown at the end of this chapter. Decide what classifications you want to use to analyse your use of time and write them at the top of the sheet, with the times of the working day down the side. Carry it with you throughout the day and note the start and finish time of every activity. For frequent small activities, such as brief telephone calls and interruptions, a simple tick is easier. Don't be afraid to be seen using it – tell people what you are doing and they will respect you for it.

Highly logical managers tend to design a log that is too complex in an effort to capture all the details. Don't try to record too much – six or eight headings are quite enough. These headings should relate to things that happen quite frequently for short periods, such as reading, interruptions and social chat. Activities such as formal meetings and travel, which occur less frequently, can be recorded under a 'miscellaneous' heading. Alternatively you can use a time log to focus on one or two particular time-wasters like interruptions.

Highly creative managers, on the other hand, skimp on detail. They prefer to use estimates, recording at the end of the day, or at the end of each hour, but this is much less accurate and may give a very distorted picture. Memory is an unreliable guide: we tend to remember the highlights, like externally imposed problems, and to underestimate easy everyday activities, like social chat and reading. Much better to record events as they happen.

At first, no doubt, you will hate me for suggesting this exercise. Filling in a time log is a painful process and you will probably discover, midway through the first day, that you have forgotten about it for the past hour. Push on – with practice it will get easier.

I do not recommend keeping a log for long – maybe one day as a trial run to help you design a system that suits you, and then two or three days to give you some factual data. When you have achieved this, try running it again for a couple of days every six months or so to monitor progress.

When you are planning your day, forecast the time you will need for all significant tasks, then review 'actual' against 'forecast'. Some jobs regularly take twice as long as expected. Would an accountant be happy with an item that regularly exceeded budget by 100 per cent? Most people find that the process of recording their use of time helps them to become more efficient before they have even analysed the results.

When you know what you are spending your time on, you can compare it with the way you ought to be spending it. Most managers spend their time even less effectively than they think they do, so time logs can be a frightening experience. In fact they are sometimes the catalyst that persuades a manager to make some fundamental changes to working methods. It might be an excellent place to start the search for greater personal effectiveness.

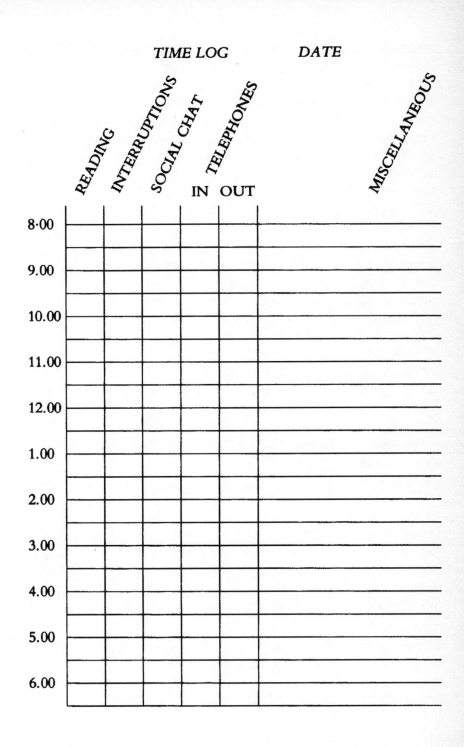

PART II
PEOPLE ISSUES

Some managers are very logical. They are good at dealing with problems which can be analysed in a rational manner, but less effective with those parts of their job which behave less logically – namely other people.

This second section is devoted to those vital high-leverage skills of dealing with other people. It starts with an analysis of the changing role of the manager and a chapter on communication skills, and goes on to look at relationships in several dimensions. These include delegation, probably the second most important key to effective time management after prioritizing, managing the boss and dealing with others. The final chapter, on 'others', uses a marketing framework to analyse relationships.

13. The Changing Role of the Manager

Once upon a time, large organizations were based upon organization charts like the one below.

Up at the top of the organization was someone who took lots of decisions, who issued orders, and who was presumed by many to be infallible, so I shall call him GOD. At the next level in the

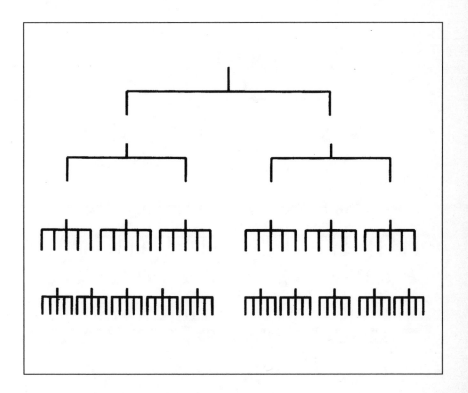

organization were people who wore seven-piece suits and had big corner offices. We didn't see them very often because they spent their time travelling the world, sitting on committees and attending dinners, but we saw their pictures in the papers from time to time. I shall call them Mr Big and Mr Important. That word 'Mr' is not a mistake, because it always was 'Mr' in those far-off times.

At the next level it became rather difficult to know exactly who did what; it all looked rather grey to those who worked at the bottom of the heap. In fact the chief distinguishing feature of the people at this next level was that these were the other people who had reserved places in the company car park; these were the other people who were allowed to eat in the executive dining room; and in one company I worked in they also peed in the executive toilet. Goodness knows what they did, but they had lots of perks and privileges, so they were obviously of some importance.

Down at the very bottom, in the front line, were large numbers of people called workers, them, the hoi polloi, the rabble, worms, plebs,

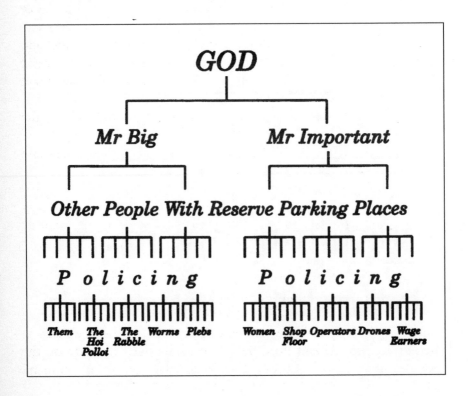

the shop floor, operators, drones, wage earners, or some other disparaging description. Oh, yes, and there were a lot of women at that level also.

What we had were hierarchical organizations, not dissimilar to those created by the Chinese 2,500 years ago, or used by the Roman Army: the people with the brains at the top, taking the decisions; the people without the brains at the bottom, obeying the orders. Wherever that type of organization has existed, the job of the first-line supervisor and junior manager has tended to be a policing job: passing orders to the front line; spying on people to see if they are obeying the orders; and reporting on them to the commanders when they aren't.

This style of organization has not been particularly successful in recent years. In fact, whenever I have found myself in any organization that is based in any way on these principles I have noticed a behaviour emerging among the front-line staff which is known as 'Malicious Compliance'. They will take great delight in following an instruction to the letter – especially when they know it is wrong.

If you cast your mind back to your school days you will probably recognize this, and some of you won't need to go nearly so far back. A manager recently told me that his boss, a natural panic merchant, had charged into his office one Monday morning shouting: 'Crisis! Crisis! I want you to write me a report on XYZ for the board meeting on Wednesday.'

'I can't possibly do that by Wednesday, I'm far too busy,' said the manager.

'Drop everything,' said the boss, 'I must have it by Wednesday,' and he walked out, slamming the door behind him.

The manager did as he was told.

On the Wednesday morning at 9.59, one minute before the start of the board meeting, his boss flew in again: 'Where are my monthly figures for the board?'

'I haven't done them.'

'You haven't done them?'

'You told me to drop everything.'

Does that sound familiar? Another of my colleagues reacted immediately to the phrase 'malicious compliance'. His face lit up as he recalled an incident from his National Service. 'We were on the parade ground, square bashing. Up, down, left, right – real command material. After 45 minutes, as we marched across the parade ground, the sergeant's attention was distracted. We made it over the edge onto the flower beds and trampled down all the flowers.'

Judging by the look on his face and the animation in his voice, this was not just the highlight of his National Service; it was one of the best days of his entire life. If *they* are so clever that they can take all the decisions, we do like to see them fall flat on their faces occasionally. Can we hope to deliver consistent quality and good service in any organization when the front-line staff feel like that?

Modern organizations are moving towards a new model. This time it does not start with some managerial god but with the people who matter most, the customers. If an organization is going to succeed, it must meet the needs of its customers, so they will be put at the top of the organization chart. Next come the people who do things for customers, the 'Front Line Staff'.

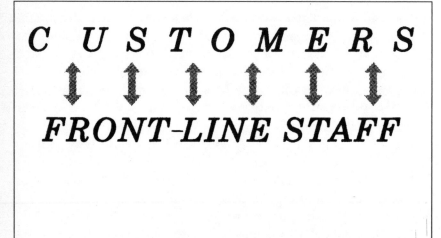

This new model for an organization can be applied to an overall organization like British Airways, or to any unit within the organization, such as the Personnel Department.

Take your own unit. It may well be that the customers served by your unit are fellow members of the same overall organization, but the model works just as well with internal customers. Assuming that your 'front line staff' want to do a good job (and, all else being equal, I believe that almost everyone *does* want to), ask yourself, 'What do my people need to enable them to do a good job?' Or, for that matter, 'What does anyone need, to enable them to do a good job?'

Answer this question yourself before reading my answers:

WHAT DO PEOPLE NEED TO ENABLE THEM TO DO A GOOD JOB?

. . . .
. . . .
. . . .
. . . .

I have put that question to many managers, and the responses tend to include the following:

- Clear objectives
- Sense of purpose
- Authority, information and trust
- Tools and equipment
- Training
- Feedback
- Support

The organization as a whole needs many other elements, such as strategy, control systems, innovation etc., but this list is a good description of the role of the manager as a leader in a modern organization. Note the complete change of emphasis from the previous description, 'Policing': no longer the manager as policeman, controller and administrator; the new manager is a coach, facilitator and encourager.

It is interesting to note that some of these 'softer' people skills are more often found in women than in men. When I look round the senior management teams of many organizations I see that they have a problem – not enough women – and I believe that they will not evolve a fully modern approach until they achieve a better balance between the sexes at the most senior levels.

The story is told of the two managers walking in the Kenyan countryside. Rounding a hillock, they suddenly saw a lion, not more than 80 paces away. They froze in terror. The lion looked at them. For a full minute, nothing moved. Then one of the managers reached slowly into his bag, pulled out a pair of running shoes, and started to put them on.

'Don't be stupid,' whispered his companion, 'You can't possibly out-run a lion.' 'I don't have to,' came the reply. 'I only have to out-run you.'

The moral of this story is that you must know who you are competing with. All too often, in the old hierarchical organizations the 'management' would be competing with the 'workers', the sales department would be competing with the production department and the whole organisation would have an almost adversarial relationship with its suppliers and its customers. The modern, customer-focused organization is based on teamwork and co-operation. Where the extreme hierarchical organization was based on the principle that every decision was taken at the highest pos-sible level, the modern customer-focused organization is based on the principle that every decision is taken as near to the front-line as possible. Where the hierarchical organization was functionally organized with most communication running up and down the organization, the modern organization is full of task groups and project teams, with much more complex communication patterns.

In this less-structured environment, the key skills required for managerial effectiveness must include those of relating to people: communication skills, delegation, leadership and working with others both within the organization and outside.

POSTSCRIPT FROM FRANCE

Empowerment is the stuff of revolution. Politically, the French Revolution transformed the masses from peasants to citizens. That is roughly what is now happening in our organizations, though we hope the change will be effected more smoothly. If we need a slogan for our employee revolution we could use one of the best from the past: 'Liberté, Egalité, Fraternité'.

Liberté, or freedom, is primarily freedom of speech, freedom of the press and thus freedom of information. Every member of the organization has a right to know what is happening. Information should not be withheld as an instrument of managerial power: it must be available to serve the people, to allow them to take intelligent decisions, to enable them to be creative and to facilitate communication. New information technologies must be used to make information available at all points of decision throughout our organizations.

Egalité, or equality, is primarily equality of opportunity – in reality and practice, not just in the policy manuals. Equality between the sexes, equality between the races and equality between the social classes, with training available for everyone and with decisions taken by those who have the knowledge and skills, rather than those with the status.

Fraternité is probably best translated as 'Solidarity'. We are all in it together. We are inter-dependent. You cannot play winning football if half the team does not give a hoot. Let us recognize that and work with it. Traditional organizations were divided into water-tight compartments, like the Titanic. There were Marketing, Sales, Operations, Finance etc., with solid walls between and not much effective communication. Cutting it horizontally we had management and workers, salaried staff and wage earners, White collar and Blue collar – again, all competing rather than co-operating.

In the future we must work more closely with our customers to discover solutions of mutual benefit to both parties; Marketing must learn to work with Operations in harmonious co-operation; and above all, management and the front-line staff must recognize and welcome the fact that they are members of the same team. A good team encourages individual dignity, meaning and a sense of community. It creates an environment in which everyone can learn and grow together as they co-operate to achieve the organization's objectives.

14. Effective Communication

Communication is a central part of our lives. Our very existence as social beings is based on communication. Genetically, the human mind has not changed significantly over the past 3,000 years. The remarkable development of our civilization has occurred because we have accumulated a vast body of knowledge which each generation has communicated to the next.

We communicate all the time, with families, friends, colleagues, customers, suppliers and others. We have all been communicating since childhood, so we ought to be experts. It is easy to see that it might be difficult to communicate with strangers, or to communicate with people in large groups, but one-to-one communication with people we know well ought to be easy.

But is it? If you have a spouse or partner, can you honestly say that you always communicate effectively? Or do problems arise even there?

The increasing complexity of relationships in customer-focused organizations will place ever greater demands on our communication skills, and yet poor communication skills are already a great cause of inefficiency in organizations, and thus a significant time-waster.

This chapter will look at seven aspects of communication:

- General principles of communication
- Written communication
- Making presentations
- Listening skills
- Persuasive communication
- Men and women talking
- Non-verbal communication

GENERAL PRINCIPLES OF COMMUNICATION

Are people good at listening to you? Do they always hear what you say and understand what you mean? Observe people talking in a bar or café and see how much of the time the non-speaker appears not to be listening. Most people do not listen very well. For part of the time when you are talking to them they are thinking of something else – often thinking of what they will say next – and when they do listen, they often misunderstand what you are saying. For a start, it is worth noting that words carry no meaning, but acquire meaning from their context: the same word in a different context may have a very different meaning.

Husbands and wives, managers, salesmen and customers, everybody tends to hear what they expect to hear, and tends not to understand messages which do not fit their expectations. What seems obvious and easy to you may not be to someone else.

The meaning of a sentence can also change dramatically with slight changes in emphasis. Try saying the following sentence putting a slight emphasis on one word, then repeat the sentence seven times putting the emphasis on a different word each time: 'I didn't say you took the red pen.'

Another area of misunderstanding exists because we tend to hear what we expect to hear and to see what we expect to see. Here is an old visual example:

PARIS
IN THE
THE SPRING

What was wrong with that? If you didn't spot it, try reading it again, very slowly, word by word.

Words which seem unimportant can go in one ear and out the other without touching the memory at all. We notice only the patterns and meanings. If I wish to communicate with you, I start with an holistic idea (which may not be clearly thought out), I translate that into a linear stream of words (which may not describe the idea accurately), I speak (but I don't always say what I mean to say) while you listen (but not all the time), and you translate the words you hear into an holistic idea. What are the chances of your ending up with an accurate copy of my original idea?

We do not hear well when we are angry, frightened, uncomfortable or in pain – and even in the best of circumstances the non-speaker is often not listening. Remember that the silent figure you are talking to, be it customer, colleague, boss, or family member, will only understand a small part of what you are trying to say. In fact the most common mistake in communication is the assumption that it has taken place.

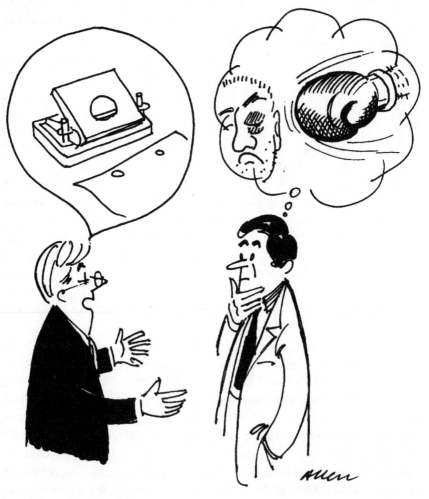

"I need a punch"

To communicate effectively with someone you must make allowances for these problems. There is sometimes a difference between the message sent and the message received. The only thing that *matters* in communication is the message that is received. At the end of a communication it does not matter what you said, even less important is what you think you said or what you meant to say – the only thing that matters is what the other person *thinks* you said.

So how can you minimize the risk of misunderstandings? There are two ways, and good communicators use both. First, make your message easy to understand, which means using the other person's language and terminology and basing the message on *their* assumptions, needs, wants and fears; second, check regularly to see whether you are being understood.

WRITTEN COMMUNICATION

Written communication is one-way communication, so there is no opportunity for immediate feedback. This makes it a weak form of communication. Sending a memo is not communication.

However, we do use a great deal of written communication, so let's make the most of it. Do you ever receive long-winded, boring 20-page reports? How do you feel as you read them?

I believe that all reports should be written for easy reading. In fact, I will go further and suggest that anything really worth saying can be put on one side of one piece of paper. If you must write 20 pages, then start with a one-page summary: this is what it's about and these are my conclusions; then treat the other 19 pages as appendices for those who need the detail.

We don't like to do this. We worry that if we give away the punchline on page one people may not read the rest – but if they don't need the rest then it is only common human decency to give it to them in that form. It may take a little longer to write a report in such a concise way, but I believe it's only when you reduce a subject down to its simplest form that you truly understand it. As Sir John Harvey-Jones puts it, 'If you cannot communicate adequately the main points that you want to get across on two sides of paper, you have almost certainly not thought the problem out properly.'

MAKING PRESENTATIONS

Some people seem to be naturally good at making presentations. This is an illusion – standing up and talking to a large group does not come naturally; it is a skill that has been acquired, and it can be acquired by anyone, even by those who are by nature shy and intro-verted. It is possible to reach a senior management position without this skill, as some senior managers prove regularly, but it becomes a definite handicap.

Imagine yourself sitting in the audience for a presentation. What are the worst offences that speakers regularly commit? Most would say 'speaking for too long' and 'being boring'. The worst speakers do both.

And what do you remember from a typical presentation? Not a lot, usually. You are most likely to remember the first few minutes and the closing remarks. You may remember some of the visual aids, and possibly an occasional point that was given great emphasis or that was particularly relevant to you. The rest you will probably have forgotten even before the speaker sits down. Remember this, next time you are preparing a presentation.

When you make a presentation, you are in the spotlight. It is an opportunity to impress people. Poor communication style can drown even the best of material, so the *way* you communicate can be even more important than *what* you communicate.

Presentation skills merit a book to themselves, but here is some simple advice on speaking for easy listening and avoiding the most common pitfalls:

- Check all equipment before you start. Make sure you know where all the switches are, that the overhead projector is clean and focused, that the pens work, that the slides are the right way up and that you have everything you need. Make sure you can see a clock, or put your watch where you can glance at it.
- First impressions are vital. Dress for the occasion, stand to speak, and start with a clear and confident opening. Never begin with an apology. Recognize that your audience will want you to do well.
- People will be most likely to remember the first and last

minutes. It is worth scripting both, to give you a clear confident start and a clean sharp ending.

- Start with an outline of the talk. This acts as a map so that your listeners know where they are going. It should include your objectives and the key stages in your presentation.

- Use simple everyday language. I resent it when a speaker uses jargon, starts to talk in meaningless initials, or sounds like the terms and conditions of a legal contract. When speaking in English to an international audience, that means using simple grammatical construction and a restricted vocabulary.

- Vary your tone of voice to give emphasis to key points and to signal changes in topic. If you wish your audience to receive your presentation with enthusiasm, you must communicate your own enthusiasm. In Japanese Kabuki theatre, a man bangs two small wood blocks on a large board at key points, and the frequency and loudness of the banging denote the importance of the point. A good speaker does the same by signalling with the voice and by regular verbal signposts, for example, '. . . but the main reason is . . .', 'There seem to be two principal options', etc.

- Maintain eye contact with your audience for at least 80 per cent of the time. Don't look over them or through them, look them in the eyes. You can't do this if you are constantly reading. I use prompt cards to keep me on track, and any key words or longer passages can be written in full on the cards for emergency use.

- Visual aids also help people to listen and take a little pressure off the presenter, but always keep them simple.

- If you get any interruptions or critical questions it is essential to handle them sympathetically. If an audience feels that one of their number has been put down, the speaker may have created a martyr and people will rally behind the victim. Legitimize the intervention. Try to understand it. It is better to be seen to be over-polite to an awkward questioner than to risk being seen by the audience as having been rude to one of their number. If you don't know the answer to a question, admit it.

- If you want to generate interaction, either during the session or at the end, warn people in advance and start the process by asking them an easy question, for example, 'Who makes presentations regularly?' 'How did you feel when you first started making them?' People who talk at their audience for half an hour and then say 'Any questions?' are usually greeted with silence.

- Beware the low-responders. If you are expecting interaction and you don't get it – if people don't laugh or respond – it doesn't mean they are not enjoying it. Some people are by nature low-reactors and others may be feeling tired. I have seen the absence of expected reaction destroy even quite experienced speakers. They race ahead to the next highlight to force a reaction, lose their structure, start repeating themselves and get visibly upset. If you find yourself speaking to a group of low-reactors make it a monologue. Cut out any inessential humour and deliver it at a steady pace.

- Never over-run your time. The audience will have forgotten 80 per cent of what you said within an hour or two, so would it matter if you missed a bit out? Far better to gain credit for finishing on time.

- People will usually thank you for a copy of the talk, or a summary at the end. They are unlikely ever to read it, but they will thank you for it.

- Always get feedback on your performance. Ask a member of the audience in advance if they will do you this kindness. Take note of it, even if it hurts. The best feedback is a video camera – you won't enjoy watching your performance again, but you might learn a lot.

- Still worried? Well, the only answer is practice. Look for opportunities to practise in any setting. If your organization has a presentation which is offered to local clubs and societies, volunteer to run it; give talks to local schools; recognize that all presenters are nervous, even the most experienced. The day I cease to be nervous is the day I should give up presenting.

LISTENING SKILLS

I suggested earlier that good communicators understand the needs and assumptions of those they are communicating with, and check their understanding. How do they do that? By asking questions, of course. And when they have asked a question, what next? They listen. Do you? Really? Most people are very poor listeners.

Imagine yourself talking, trying to persuade a colleague from another department, let's call him David, to change one of his systems. You have made your plea and David is starting to respond. You listen very carefully to the first few words he says because you are interested. It becomes apparent very rapidly that he is not agreeing to your request, so you start thinking what to say next. It is impossible to think and listen at the same time, so you have stopped listening. Every 10 or 15 seconds you listen to a few words to make sure he is still saying the same thing. Eventually, when you have worked out your next statement, you may disappear into your mind again and have a little rehearsal. Then you start to listen much more closely to David, but you are concentrating on the rhythm of his speech, waiting for a pause that will allow you to make your point. If, when you try to speak, David says, 'No, let me finish first,' and talks for another three minutes, you will then take him right back to where he was before, because you haven't listened to a word of it.

What a pantomime!

Many managers are very poor listeners, yet the skill of listening is a vital element in effective communication and, like other skills, it can be developed through training and practice. The first problem is that we don't see it as a problem. How often do you see courses on 'effective listening'?

Good listening is one of the most important management skills. Listening to someone is the ultimate mark of respect. It shows that you value them – that you respect them as a person. True dialogue cannot take place without this humility. It requires mutual trust, and that takes time to develop.

Everyone is the star of their own show, everyone values their own ideas, you can't build trust with anyone unless they feel understood. Notice that the important point is not just that you should understand them, but that they should feel understood.

Oppression can be defined as the failure to treat people as people, and it starts by not listening to them. Not listening is an insult – and clever people often don't listen. They play a game of 'I know more than you', scoring points by talking. Every time they win this battle, they lose the war.

I was sitting in front of a CCTV monitor one day with a young Japanese manager, watching a group of European managers in a 'team working' exercise. Within minutes they were all talking at once – well, shouting actually, arguing with one another.

The Japanese manager said, 'I thought they were supposed to be friends.'

'Yes,' I replied. 'They are.'

'But they are arguing,' said the Japanese manager.

'I am afraid that's what often happens in the West,' I replied.

'Do you mean the same thing will be happening in the other groups?'

'I'm afraid so,' I said.

'Can I go and see?'

'Certainly.'

He returned a few minutes later, wide-eyed in disbelief: 'In Japan we have a saying. If you want to be heard, first you must listen to the other person.'

What a good idea!

Try answering the following two questions in relation to your boss, to a colleague, to your secretary and to your children or other family members.

- How much time and energy do you put into making yourself understood?
- How much time and energy do you put into understanding the other person?

Active Listening

Active listening means not just hearing what is being said, but encouraging and helping the speaker to speak. It involves *showing* that you are listening, *sounding* as though you are listening, proving regularly that you have *heard* what has been said and, where appropriate, letting the other person *know* that you understand how they are feeling.

You can show that you are listening by sitting in an active position, leaning slightly forward, with eyes wide open and focused for most of the time on the speaker's face. You can sound as though you are listening by making 'continuity' noises while the other person is speaking, for example . . . 'yes' . . . 'yes' . . . 'yes' . . . 'really' . . . 'then what happened?' . . . These noises are particularly important in telephone communication where visual signals are absent.

You can check that you have heard what has been said and prove that you have been listening by summarizing from time to time, for example, 'So if I understand you rightly, what you are saying is that you couldn't complete the report on time because of the number of interruptions you received.'

Active listening means suppressing your own thoughts and views, resisting the temptation to interrupt, to advise, to evaluate, to tell stories, and focusing on understanding the other person. Accept the possibility that there could be more than one view of reality and use objective open questions to explore the other person's mind. If you have one view and I have another and if we manage to communicate these fully to one another, one of us may learn something. It might be you.

Most people like to talk and you are showing them personal respect by listening to them. You will also be helping them to relax, and thus to think clearly and to express themselves. Not only does listening help to build relationships but you will also gather a lot of useful information, which you can never do while you are talking.

As a manager go and listen to your people; As a parent, go and listen to your children. It might be the best thing you can do for them.

Why do we find listening so difficult?
A few pages ago I used the word 'humility' – not the most common of managerial characteristics. Many of us learned, at school, that we should be strong and that we should know all the answers. Teachers knew all the answers – but then they also asked all the questions, and they only asked questions to which they already knew the answers. The world of work isn't like that. There are many things we don't know, and we should feel no shame in admitting it. Having to be right all the time and knowing all the answers is very exhausting, and it is a colossal barrier to learning.

Many managers like to be in control: when they are talking they feel in control. When they are involved in genuine two-way conversations they feel threatened.

Many managers suffer from premature evaluation. They evaluate and judge what they hear and start reacting to it, in their mind if not out loud. You can't think and listen simultaneously, and since we think much faster than we speak, our thoughts are often more interesting than what is being said, so we stop listening.

Many of us feel that we don't have time to listen.

Practising Listening

If you suspect that you could improve your listening skills, there are countless opportunities to do so. You can practise in social situations as well as at work. Here are some simple guidelines:

- Plan before any interaction, jotting down any questions you want to ask so that you will not need to think during the conversation.

- For a business meeting, take a pad with you and jot down any distracting thoughts that cross your mind so that you can clear your head for listening. (You may sometimes find that these jottings are rather more interesting than the notes of the meeting, which is a bonus).

- Focus your entire energy on understanding the other person before you start to judge. This is especially important where you disagree with what is being said. It means suppressing your emotions and focusing on exploring their views and the reasons for them, asking the follow-up questions that can reveal so much: 'Why did that happen?', 'You didn't seem too sure about that,' 'When do you think that will be?'

- If you normally speak too much, try to say only what will help the others. Ask yourself whether the others will want to hear it, and whether it must be said now. Note down your thoughts and give others a chance to speak first.

- Summarize what the other person has said to check that you have understood properly – they will almost invariably tell you more. End a meeting by summarizing the other person's viewpoint.

- Recognize that it takes considerable self-confidence to be open to the ideas of others. Are you up to it? (This is especially true when hearing things we don't like, or getting personal feedback.)

Three questions for you

Imagine two people: one a very wise person, the other a very foolish person. What do these words mean? Well, 'wise' does not mean having two university degrees. Many well-qualified people are far from being wise. Maybe 'street wise' is a better definition, and 'foolish' is the opposite of wise.

These two people spend time together, maybe on a train, and they have a conversation. Which of them do you think will learn most as a result of the conversation, and why?

Most people think that the wise person will learn, and suggest that wisdom had to do with the ability to learn: and you can always learn something from somebody else, however foolish, because their experience is different. 'Foolishness', on the other hand, is even more certainly related to the inability to learn.

Next question: if you agree that the wise person is more likely to learn, will the learning occur primarily by talking, or by listening? And the answer must, of course, be 'listening'.

Final question: in your organization and in your family, who does the talking and who does the listening?

PERSUASIVE COMMUNICATION

When two people wish to communicate with one another the first step is to establish rapport, to get the conversation under way and help both parties feel comfortable. Some people do this with lengthy rituals about the weather, the state of business, or last night's TV programmes. Others prefer to get down to business rather faster.

If you wish to communicate effectively with another person, try to adapt to their preferred pattern, find out where they are coming from and meet them there. When two people have established close rapport they seem to match one another's behaviour in many ways. They both lean forward, and back at the same time. They both cross their legs, they both take a drink. If you could listen in, you would find that they were speaking at the same speed and using similar language and imagery. This is the way we behave when we have close rapport, and skilled communicators have learned how to simulate it.

With rapport, a conversation is like a game of catch. It is a co-operative game in which both parties share the talking, and both show a genuine interest in what the other has to say.

Without rapport it is difficult to convey any but the simplest messages.

Having established rapport, the next stage in a conversation is often to discover the other person's views or needs. Questioning is the key still here, but again it is sometimes mis-handled. If I ask

111

people, 'Why might your boss ask you a question?' many of the responses I get are along these lines:

- To check on me
- To catch me out
- To put me under pressure

Questioning without rapport can all too easily become an inquisition. Far better to establish the objective of the discussion first and then encourage the other person to talk.

Since effective communication is so difficult, considerable effort should be put into checking whether it has taken place. One of the most useful of behaviours in communications is summarizing. When someone has made a point to you, summarize what they have said back to them. Likewise, use questions to check whether people have understood you and, if they haven't, be humble enough to recognize that it is your fault. We need this feedback, but when it shows that the other person hasn't understood we don't like it.

Questions can also be a very useful way of taking the pressure off yourself. When I am 'negotiating', I always jot down a few questions in advance so that I will be free to listen properly. If I suddenly find that I am expected to speak, I can glance down and find a question to ask. In negotiations it is also important to avoid taking firm positions early on. Much better: 'There are a great many advantages of open-plan offices,' rather than: 'It must be an open-plan office.' Likewise, don't let the other person dig themselves into a hole. If John says, 'I insist on having a private office,' you might reply, 'Well I can see that you feel strongly about this, let's list the advantages and disadvantages.' If someone disagrees strongly with what you have said, ask them to summarize the point they are disagreeing with. As often as not they will have misunderstood it.

The process of persuasive communication is a very sophisticated form of personal interaction. It is far more complex than making a presentation. Indeed, it has often been said that 'Telling is not Selling'. If that is so, then why do so many people spend so much time *telling*? Well, the main reason is that it is much easier and more natural to talk and tell, and much harder work to question and listen. Telling gives the illusion of control and dominance: once again people fall for the easy and pleasant at the expense of the effective.

The basic format of conversation should be:

- Establish rapport
- Discover the other person's views and needs
- Explain your own position
- Explore all possible options
- Negotiate
- Agree

MEN AND WOMEN TALKING

I can recommend a seminal book on the subject of verbal communication: *You Just Don't Understand*, by Deborah Tannen (Virago, 1991). She examines the different ways the two sexes approach conversation – which accounts for much of the misunderstanding that occurs in both business and personal relationships and contributes to male dominance in both.

NON-VERBAL COMMUNICATION

Most of the message received comes from non-verbal cues.

You can learn a great deal about a person simply by watching them, without hearing what they are saying. People display their character and motivation through their gestures, facial expressions and body and eye movements and tone of voice. Other people receive these non-verbal messages. Many of the people you meet will receive such messages from you. Are they the messages you would wish them to receive?

Non-verbal communication is an important part of all interpersonal communication – and especially of selling. Much is known about interpreting non-verbal signals, but it is too much of a specialist subject for this book, and much non-verbal behaviour varies between cultures.

It is exceedingly difficult to control our non-verbal signals. The best way to ensure that these non-verbal messages agree with your verbal communication is to believe in what you are saying and to feel it is important. Adopt an open posture, use frequent eye contact and soften your face – smile!

Try a little experiment to test the power of non-verbal signals:

adopt a solemn face and look at yourself in the mirror; then, very slowly, start to smile, and see what effect it has on you.

LESSONS FOR LIFE

Clearly all that has been said in this chapter applies to family and other non-work relationships. I usually try to resist offering advice, but if there is one suggestion I would like to commend to the average male manager, it is to go home and listen, really listen, to your partner and your children. You will be amazed at the effect on your relationships, and you might even learn something.

SUMMARY

It has been said that, 'Nobody ever sold anyone anything. The task is to help them to buy.' Likewise, 'Nobody every taught anyone anything, the task is to help them to learn.' A good communicator, whether salesperson, manager, colleague or parent, will constantly put themselves in the shoes of the person they are communicating with, seeing everything from their point of view.

This chapter has yielded a rich crop of new time-wasters which must be added to the list:

TIME-WASTERS

Poor sense of time
Inability to say 'No'
OVER-LENGTHY REPORTS
BORING PRESENTATIONS
TALKING TOO MUCH
RELUCTANCE TO ASK SIMPLE QUESTIONS
PRETENDING TO KNOW
NOT LISTENING
PREMATURE EVALUATION
RESISTANCE TO FEEDBACK
POOR RAPPORT SKILLS

15. Delegation

Since this book is being written primarily for managers, it is high time I offered a definition of management: 'Management is getting things done through others.' Crude and simplistic as it is, I think most people would accept that as a basic definition.

If managing is 'getting things done through others' it can be contrasted with 'doing things yourself' – if you are doing it yourself you are not managing, managing is getting things done through others. It suggests the act of *delegation*. The simple chart below shows what happens as you progress though your career as a manager.

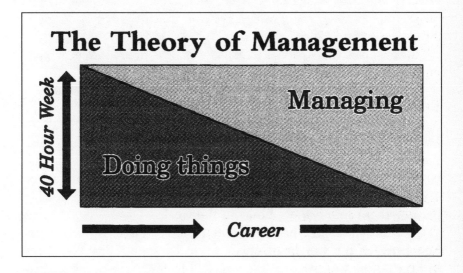

When you started work, in some front-line job, you probably spent 40 hours a week – or however many hours there were – 'doing things'.

At the level of first-line supervision or junior management, much of the week is still spent doing things but a small part is spent managing. The further you climb the managerial hierarchy the higher the proportion of your time that is spent managing and the lower the proportion that is spent doing.

That is the theory. Unfortunately it is rarely borne out in practice. What usually happens ends up looking more like this:

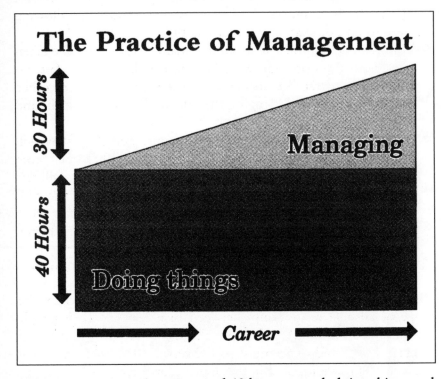

Many managers continue to spend 40 hours a week doing things and the time needed for managing has to be added on, causing the working week to get longer and longer. At somewhere around 65 or 70 hours a week they hit a limit. They are no longer promotable because there are no more hours in the week.

I remind you of the principle stated earlier: 'There is no correlation between the weight of organizational responsibility you carry and the amount of personal time needed to discharge that responsibility.' The answer to effectiveness is and always must be *leverage*. Successful delegation is one of the principal sources of leverage available to managers. It is an area rich in opportunities, yet fraught with danger and traps. It is an area that is frequently mis-handled by managers at all levels, but effective delegation is a skill which can be learned.

BENEFITS OF EFFECTIVE DELEGATION

- Effective delegation will free you to devote more time to your high-leverage tasks, thereby increasing your effectiveness as a manager, increasing your chances of promotion and allowing you to go home at a more sensible time.
- Effective delegation will mean that many decisions will be taken nearer to the front-line. Such decisions will always be faster – and often better – than decisions taken in a manager's office (even yours), thus improving the effectiveness of your unit and reinforcing your promotability.
- Your people will enjoy being given more authority, they will grow and develop as individuals and thus become more motivated, more committed and more skilful. Not only will this further contribute to the success of your unit, but you will acquire a nice inner glow of satisfaction that comes from knowing that you have been able to help a fellow human being.

ACQUIRING LEVERAGE THROUGH DELEGATION

Delegation is not a matter of yes or no, it is not an on/off switch. The range of possible relationships between managers and their people can be put on a sliding scale, from the most autocratic and lowest leverage at one end to the most participative and highest leverage at the other. This is illustrated in the drawing over the page.

On this scale I suggest that 'management' starts in the middle. Below that you would not be 'managing': at best you would be the overseer, giving out the tasks; at worst a dictator ordering people around.

Management has to be more than that. If you wish to be a manager, train your people always, always to come to you with *recommendations*, not with problems. This is the start of leverage. It means that they arrive with the brain in gear; they think before they come, and when they do that, they find they can often answer the problem themselves without needing to bother you. Even when they do come, it will set up the meeting as a coaching session and coaching is a high leverage activity. When someone says, 'I've got a problem,' it's just so tempting and we help them. Helping is a low leverage activity.

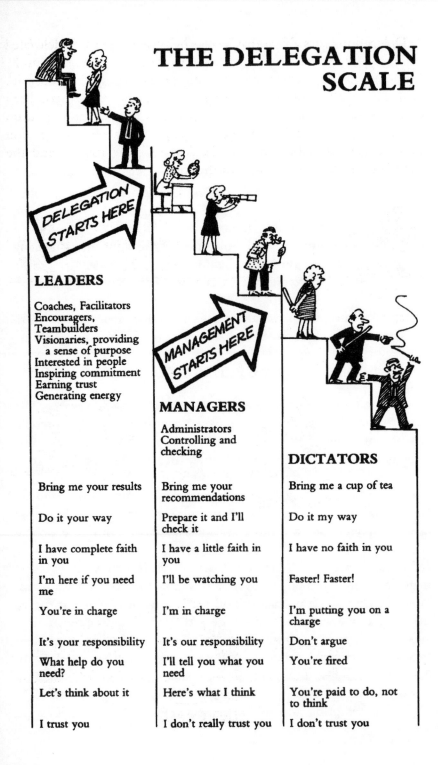

THE DELEGATION SCALE

DELEGATION STARTS HERE

LEADERS

Coaches, Facilitators
Encouragers,
Teambuilders
Visionaries, providing
  a sense of purpose
Interested in people
Inspiring commitment
Earning trust
Generating energy

MANAGEMENT STARTS HERE

MANAGERS

Administrators
Controlling and
checking

DICTATORS

LEADERS	MANAGERS	DICTATORS
Bring me your results	Bring me your recommendations	Bring me a cup of tea
Do it your way	Prepare it and I'll check it	Do it my way
I have complete faith in you	I have a little faith in you	I have no faith in you
I'm here if you need me	I'll be watching you	Faster! Faster!
You're in charge	I'm in charge	I'm putting you on a charge
It's your responsibility	It's our responsibility	Don't argue
What help do you need?	I'll tell you what you need	You're fired
Let's think about it	Here's what I think	You're paid to do, not to think
I trust you	I don't really trust you	I don't trust you

Delegation starts above that level – because you haven't delegated until you have given someone the authority to act without consulting you first. Start a new recruit with 'prepare it and I'll check it', with the objective of moving them up the scale as soon as you both feel comfortable. Start a new responsibility for an existing team member in the middle, again moving up the scale as soon as you both feel comfortable, and for the low-risk, the routine and the mundane, in due course right to the top.

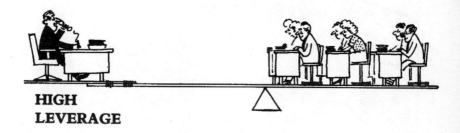

**HIGH
LEVERAGE**

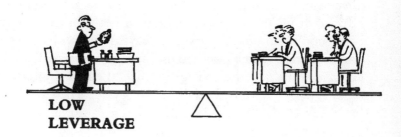

**LOW
LEVERAGE**

**NO
LEVERAGE**

Never, ever drop below the level of 'management' unless the building is on fire. In an outright crisis, the rules can change, but as soon as the crisis is over, ask yourself, 'What can I do to make sure that crisis does not occur again?'

Delegation is central to the process of acquiring leverage, so its importance rises the further up the organization you go. But since delegation is implicit in the concept of management, the principles apply everywhere in the organization. Without delegation, any managerial job becomes arduous and exhausting. When a manager fails to delegate to her people:

- They don't have the authority or the information to take decisions.
- They don't have the self-confidence to take decisions.
- They are afraid of criticism.
- In an effort to avoid all risk, they delegate back to the manager at the slightest opportunity – she ends up trying to do their jobs and becomes chronically overloaded. People can always be seen popping in to managers like this with minor problems. The manager, being too busy at the moment, usually responds 'leave that with me'. After a while, the manager runs out of time and her people run out of work. This leaves them with only one line of approach: to supervise their manager. You will find them coming back into the manager's office to check up from time to time – 'Any progress with those dates yet?', 'Have you managed to speak to the customer?', etc. What a pantomime. I do hope your people never have to do that to you.

In extreme cases the manager knows that she is holding up her people, feels guilty about it and hides from them. This is a natural human reaction. If I had borrowed £10 from you yesterday, then this morning, still with no money in my pockets, I saw you approaching in the distance, what would I do? I might well feel guilty and try to avoid you. When bosses start avoiding their people the relationship is in trouble. You cannot run an organization like that.

Turn the tables on your people. Recognize that the way to gain more authority is to begin to give it away. Learn the art of delegation and become a real manager. Spend time with your people. Spend lots of time with them but spend it:

- Coaching
- Counselling
- Motivating
- Agreeing objectives

These are all high-leverage activities. Do not do their jobs, that is low-leverage.

On the other hand, delegation must not be dumping, or giving others all the dirty jobs. It must not be abdication, or walking away and ignoring them. It must be a continually evolving relationship.

The potential benefits of delegation are enormous, the procedure is simple, so why is delegation so often a problem? The reason, once more, is that the road to effective delegation is lined with a wide array of temptations and traps. I have identified several but no doubt there are more. The major ones are as follows:

NINE EXCUSES FOR POOR DELEGATION

- Delegation is risky
- My people are idiots
- Doing is more fun than managing
- I can do it better
- I am an expert
- It is quicker to do it myself
- I like doing that job
- Helping people
- My people are overloaded

And three reasons that are harder to spot

- Showing off
- Insecurity
- Unclear boundaries

Delegation is risky
When I ask managers why they are reluctant to delegate, the first answer usually relates to risk: 'They might make a mess of it,' 'It's safer to do it myself,' etc. It is true that there is always an element of

risk in delegation. You can delegate the responsibility for a task to someone, you can make them accountable to you for successfully accomplishing that task, but you cannot delegate your own accountability. You will be held accountable for the performance of your entire team. If they make a mistake, you must take the blame.

But this should not be used as an *excuse* for failing to delegate. You must take steps to *limit* the risk. Consider, again, the scale used earlier. At the top ('Do it your way'), risk is at its greatest, so this is used only for the low-risk areas of the job and the tried and trusted team members. But the middle point ('Do it and I'll check it') is risk free. You have eliminated risk. So risk, alone, cannot be a valid reason for lack of delegation.

My people are idiots

Some people have very little faith in their fellow human beings; they have an almost neurotic need to be in control of everything. They don't even like being a passenger in a car driven by someone else. They tend to become petty tyrants or dictators at work – and sometimes also at home. They can be perfectionists, who insist that everything is done exactly as they want it. When they do try to delegate, they end up hovering over people's shoulders, fussing and criticizing. They transfer to themselves some responsibility for what their people do. If this pattern of behaviour continues for long enough, the brighter people leave and those who stay learn to avoid taking responsibility. With no feeling of involvement and no chance to influence, they become apathetic, thus confirming the manager's original views.

It's hard to hand over the steering wheel when you think you are the only one who can drive! When you delegate, things will not be done exactly in your way. You must learn to tolerate these differences because you cannot afford the luxury of getting involved in the detail. It is said that there are no bad soldiers, only bad generals. Lack of faith in others becomes a self-fulfilling prophecy.

Doing is more fun than managing

When you are doing something yourself it is exciting and rewarding. You can see the results at once. When you are managing, you are further from the action. This is another example of the earlier traps 'fire fighting is fun' and 'immediate reward'. If managing is to be a high-leverage activity, the real rewards will come in the long term and managers must learn to wait for them.

I can do it better

Managers who are promoted within a function can often do their previous job, in which they have had years of experience, better than the new person who has just replaced them. It is also likely that they will be able to do their previous job better than their new one. However, if they persist in this activity they will ruin two jobs simultaneously – their own and their successor's.

I am an expert

For those who spend their early careers as technical experts, managing is often an irritating sideshow that interferes with their real work. Such people can face a difficult decision as managerial duties grow: do you want to continue as The Technical Expert, in which case you should allow someone else to take up the managerial role; or do you want to become a professional manager, in which case you will probably need some management training and will have to recognize that others will become The Technical Experts. (J Sainsbury approach this problem by moving managers sideways into a new department so that they can no longer be The Expert in the job and are forced to concentrate on management.)

There are many situations where people would be right to choose to remain a technical expert, particularly where the technical expertise is vital, as in scientific research, or where the person concerned is unlikely to become an effective manager. Many a sales department has been doubly weakened by having its best sales person become a poor sales manager. In such situations organizations should develop parallel promotion ladders so that those who choose to continue as technical experts can gain the full reward for their contribution without being forced into managerial roles to which they may not be well suited.

It is quicker to do it myself

If I can do a job in ten minutes, which would take Peter two hours, should I do it? No. Try this approach: sit down with Peter and say, 'I would like to make this part of your job. I would like you to take responsibility for this aspect of our operations. Now I know that will be difficult for you to start with, because I have always done it myself up to now. Take it away, work out what you think you should do with it, come back at 11 o'clock tomorrow and we'll talk about it. Let's operate like that until the end of the month – by then I hope that you will have the confidence to deal with it without the need to consult me first. Are you happy with that?' And I think he will be.

If the boss or the client is standing in the doorway shouting for action NOW, then you may have to do it yourself. But that sounds like a Grade One Panic, and as soon as the panic is over you must ask yourself: 'What can I do to avoid getting into that situation again?' . . . and you are back talking to Peter.

I like doing that job
Sometimes bosses fail to delegate a task because they enjoy it too much. These people tend to delegate only boring and unpleasant tasks, with obvious effects on their people's job satisfaction.

Helping people
Over the years I have met many people who have complained about their bosses. 'My boss doesn't trust me.' 'She's always interfering and changing things.' 'He never lets me get on with the job.' Occasionally I have had the opportunity to give some feedback to the boss in question, and the reaction is always the same: 'But I'm only trying to help.' I've come to believe that helping people is a very dangerous motivation.

Helping people often stems from a desire to be liked, and a belief that the way to be liked is to be kind and helpful. Unfortunately, 'helping' can sometimes become stifling; it implies a lack of faith in people and it can deprive people of the opportunity to learn and grow almost as effectively as the insecure manager, although with the best of intentions. In an extreme situation the junior member does all the hard work on a project, gathering the information and ploughing through the paperwork then, just as it's getting interesting, the boss comes along and 'helps' him by taking it away.

If you ask managers to define the ideal boss they will usually describe someone who is tough but fair; someone who, above all, is a good delegator; not someone who shields their staff from responsibility but who helps them to grow and develop.

Helping people is a very worthy intention, but much of what is done in the name of helping is done to bolster the ego of a weak boss and deprives others of opportunities to grow and develop.

My people are overloaded

That's fair enough. There is a limit to the amount of work that can be given to any one individual. If your people are sinking under the weight of delegated responsibilities while you are sitting at a clear desk, wondering what to do next, maybe you should reconsider the allocation.

But is that really the case? Or could it be that the overloaded people are themselves having some problems with time management? Let's ask them:

'What are your time-wasters at work?'

'What stops you being more effective?'

On the assumption that most people face roughly similar problems, their response will probably be along the following lines:

INTERRUPTIONS
MEETINGS
TELEPHONES
CRISES AND PANICS
THE BOSS

The Boss? Who is that? It must be you!

Do you ever interrupt your people?

Are you ever the source of crises and panics?

Do you dump unpleasant tasks on them?

You are not in a position to give honest and balanced responses to those questions. Only your people can answer them. Remember that good staff only stay with someone who uses them well.

Do you allow your staff to manage their time? Do you respect their priorities and avoid interrupting them – or do you add to their pressure? Do you act as a good role model in the way you manage your own time? What do you do to help them feel in control of their own jobs?

There is a limit to the amount of work any one person can accomplish, but it is only when you have satisfied yourself that you have done everything you can to help them to do things for themselves that I would accept 'overloading' as a valid long-term reason for not delegating. And even then, there are usually other colleagues around who will be only too pleased to take on some responsibilities if approached in the right way.

Showing off

This is particularly hard to spot in yourself, so I shall assume that it doesn't apply to any readers of this book. However, you may have met managers who like to demonstrate their considerable skills to their people, strutting around like some sort of managerial peacocks.

Such people have a vested interest in maintaining a differential between their own skills and those of their people: they also tend to grab the credit for any successes.

Insecurity

Others, also not represented among the readers of this book, are insecure people who withhold key pieces of information from their people in an effort to make themselves indispensable. One unfortunate side effect of this policy is that they can never take holidays for longer than one week.

Such people also worry that their people might outstrip them and take over their job, so they have a vested interest in not developing them.

If you believe that through no fault of your own you are genuinely indispensable, try asking your people what bits of your job they would like to take responsibility for. You might be surprised.

If, under your guiding hand, one of your people develops so much as to overtake you, then I define that as success. If you can achieve that regularly, you should gain recognition as that most valuable member of any team: the manager who is good at bringing people on, helping others grow and develop.

Unclear boundaries

Sometimes someone will walk into your office with a problem that is yours – fine, take it. But how will you know whether it's your problem or theirs? The only way to know is when there is a clear dividing line between your job and theirs – I suppose it's called a job description.

There will be times when you are away and one of your people has to stand in for you, or they may be on holiday and you will have to do parts of their job, but there does need to be a clear dividing line so that everyone knows what they are responsible for. Unclear boundaries are a source of much friction, inefficiency and demotivation.

A lot of our old friends have surfaced again in this chapter, including perfectionism, easy jobs and immediate reward, but there are eight new time-wasters to be added to the list:

TIME-WASTERS

Resistance to feedback
Poor rapport skills
LACK OF CONFIDENCE IN PEOPLE
NEED TO FEEL IN CONTROL
FAILURE TO DEVELOP PEOPLE
UNCLEAR BOUNDARIES
IDENTITY CRISIS
NEED TO BE LIKED
MY PEOPLE HAVE TROUBLE WITH THEIR BOSS
SHOWING OFF
INSECURITY

SECRETARIES

At the start of this chapter on delegation I suggested that 'management is getting things done through others'. One of the key members of this category 'others' is your secretary. I was dubious about the value of writing a separate section about secretaries; partly because the job of the secretary is disappearing, but more because I don't want to reinforce the view of some managers that secretaries are somehow different from other team members. I decided to include it, but to use it to illustrate the general principles of delegation, using the secretary as an *example*.

Senior executives usually have more secretarial support than more junior managers – not because they need waiting on hand and foot, not because they dictate more letters, but because they have learned to delegate properly and can thus make full use of their people. Indeed, a good personal assistant can be absolutely essential to an effective executive.

Some managers claim with pride that their secretaries *organize* them, but this is a very limited and defeatist approach to management. A secretary can only be effective when working for an organized manager. If you yourself are organized and effective, your secretary can provide invaluable assistance.

It is important not to use members of your team as a dump for unpleasant tasks, nor display lack of confidence in them, nor disrupt them. In particular a secretary should not be treated as a personal servant, asked (told?) to book theatre tickets and squash courts, to run errands etc. Each time you give the instruction: 'Do it like this,' you undermine your secretary's self-confidence. Each time you interrupt her with additional little tasks you are saying, 'Your priorities and schedules are not important.' How would you like it if your boss did that to you? Allowing others to interrupt while you are meeting with your secretary or entertaining visitors and failing to introduce her as a person reinforces any feeling of inferiority. Do you really want to lower the self-confidence of such an important team-member in this way?

One of our problems may lie in the language we use. I have avoided the word 'subordinate' in this chapter – it is a hierarchical word with classist and elitist undertones. It suggests subservience and dependency, 'belonging to an inferior rank'. Its emotive qualities are entirely negative. You would not like to be put in this category, so don't inflict it on others. In a modern organization each individual's contribution is essential to the team's success. We must develop a vocabulary that reflects this. The word 'secretary' conveys an impression of 'a person employed to assist in correspondence' which, I believe, makes it difficult for us to recognize the larger opportunities. As executives gradually learn to use the keyboards on their desks, some traditional secretarial duties are declining. You might consider a new job title, such as 'Office Manager', to help everyone recognize the secretary's changing role.

The real difference between a typist and an office manager lies in the degree of freedom the person has to act independently on their own initiative. Sit down with your office manager and discuss what should be your job and what should be hers. She might take responsibility for:

● Designing and running the filing system

- Screening all telephone calls by finding out the nature of the caller's business and, where you are not immediately available, arranging a suitable time for you to speak to the person
- Screening all mail
- Replying to some correspondence. Personally, I do not ask anyone to compose a letter to go out in my name. I believe that if someone receives a letter from me, it should be from me. I get irritated by my bank where people who write to me never seem to know what they have written. An alternative is to ask someone to reply in their own name, along the lines of 'Martin has asked me to write to you and explain that . . .'
- Organizing your appointments
- Research
- Or almost anything

The precise choice of responsibilities will depend on the nature of your job and on the two of you. What matters, though, is that you follow the basic principles of delegation:

- Delegate *objectives*, not *tasks*
- Agree performance standards and reporting procedures
- Give people the information they need to do their jobs. In the case of your office manager, that means keeping her up to date with your plans at all times, so that she is in a position to deal intelligently with everyone who wants to contact you
- Spend time with each of your people. For your office manager, meetings will need to be frequent and planned in advance – possibly half an hour at the start of each day that you are in the office, and a pre-arranged phone call each day that you are away
- Spend some of that time coaching, counselling, building commitment and, above all, raising self-confidence. This also means discussing your relationship occasionally and asking your people what you could do to make their jobs more interesting or to help them be more effective
- Make sure other members of the organization know how important each of your people is, especially your office manager
- And a special point for men. Women like to work with *real* people, not with automatons. They like to be asked how they are and what their weekend was like. You won't lose face by being

human. Respect does not come from wearing a dark suit and a stern face, it is gained by being an effective, efficient and considerate colleague

In most organizations there is a reservoir of undervalued and underused potential amongst the secretarial staff; of people who are capable of learning, developing and taking on greater responsibilities. Make the most of these opportunities.

A PERSONAL EXAMPLE

I used to have a secretary who was good at running courses, excellent in a crisis, but who couldn't type. Whenever she typed something there were always mistakes in it, so I regarded her as incompetent and she probably saw me as a complainer – it was not the best of relationships.

When she left, I applied the principles of delegation. My new 'secretary' was to be called 'Course Administrator'. At the recruitment interview I explained that one of the responsibilities I wanted her to accept was to check everything she typed for me. Not just to type it accurately, but to check it, and I asked her if she was prepared to accept that responsibility. She was.

We have a clear agreement now. I will check anything she asks me to check, if she is uncertain, but 80 per cent of what she types I don't check. I just sign the letters and she sends them out.

Now if there is a mistake in a letter with my name on it, it is my head that is on the block. You can make someone responsible to you, but you can't delegate your own responsibility. So what I must do is:

- Make sure she knows and accepts that checking is her job
- Make sure she is trained and capable of doing it
- Make sure she is motivated and trying to do it
- And then the big one: I must trust her

The final stage may be the hardest, but it is also implicit in the process of delegation. In fact some dictionaries define the word 'delegate' as 'to entrust to another'. Delegation is a gift of trust and in a climate of trust, people are likely to respond to such a challenge.

Trust is one of our greatest values. It brings out the best in people, but it does take time.

Many managers are emotionally under-developed, and don't realize the effect of the low trust environments they create. The key is to create a climate where learning is encouraged, and in which people want to take responsibility.

LESSONS FOR LIFE

'Delegation' seems a harsh word to use in a family setting, but the principles of clarifying boundaries and being a leader rather than a dictator certainly apply. For example, the endless battles over untidy bedrooms sour many a family. At a certain age, why not suggest: 'Let's stop these arguments. You can decorate your bedroom as you want, and keep it in whatever state you like, and we won't complain. That can be your territory, not ours. But if you want it to be cleaned, it must be tidy, and if you want your clothes to be washed, they must be in the laundry basket. How do you feel about that as a package?'

This way you are gaining agreement to clear objectives and then coaching, encouraging and motivating, rather than policing.

If a child is doing something of which you disapprove, in an area which is the child's responsibility, by all means let them know of your concern, but allow them to make their own decisions. Every time a parent (or a manager) uses force to compel, they win submission at the expense of the relationship. A classic case of winning the battle but losing the war.

16. The Manager as Leader

SETTING OBJECTIVES

Everybody needs to know what he or she is supposed to be doing. The mistake some managers make is to spell out exactly what they want their people to do, and *precisely* how they must do it. If you do that, you are asking your people to obey orders, to become implementers, and that is a boring job; it leaves no room for initiative. Besides, if you tell someone exactly how to do something in 12 detailed stages, the instructions become so complicated that they are almost certain to fail.

Always delegate in terms of objectives. Explain to people what they should achieve in terms of *outcome*, and leave them a little freedom to decide exactly how to achieve those outcomes. Remember, there are probably 50 ways to achieve an objective, some of which have not yet been invented. There is no reason why your favourite method should necessarily be the best.

This principle also applies to job design. The people you manage need meaningful jobs that are separate from your job. When you are absent someone will stand in for you and do part of your job, and when one of your people is on holiday you may have to do part of that job, but there does need to be a clear dividing line between your job and those of each of your people. Without that they become just 'assistant to' – and that can be a miserable job.

GAINING COMMITMENT

No amount of authority and policing can guarantee good service and quality. You might force people to say 'Have a nice day', but you cannot force them to mean it. Customers will know whether they mean it, and it's only good service when they do. In a modern organization the chief determinant of quality is not authority but *commitment*.

Some 300 years ago, a gentleman riding into London saw a stone-mason at the roadside, chipping away at a large block of stone. Later that day, as the horseman left the City, he noticed the mason, still working hard at his block of stone. The same scene was repeated twice each day for a whole week. By the Friday afternoon, the gentleman had become fascinated. He dismounted and watched for 15 minutes as the mason worked, totally absorbed in his task. Eventually the gentleman spoke: 'Excuse me, what are you doing there?' The mason looked up with pride in his face, and replied, 'I am helping Christopher Wren to build a cathedral.'

If people are to be committed to their objectives they must know not only what they are supposed to achieve, but *why*, and that overall objective must be one that they can support. It must be a worthy objective in their eyes. It should not focus on financial criteria: profit may be vital to the business, but your people will not be *inspired* by the objective of increased profit for the owners or shareholders. The one legitimate objective which just might inspire them and win their commitment is serving their customers, making their customers happy. In this way customer-focus can energize the whole organization.

FEEDBACK SYSTEMS

Everyone needs feedback: without feedback, it is hard to improve. The best feedback is direct feedback – you can see the results of your own actions. This is what you get when you hit a golf ball or bake a cake.

One of the tasks of the manager is, therefore, to set up systems that let each person get direct feedback on the outcomes they have achieved.

MANAGEMENT SUPPORT AND FEEDBACK

Picture a couple, married for ten years, sitting by the fire. The wife looks at her husband and says, 'Darling, you never tell me that you love me.' The husband, looking up from his paper, says firmly, 'I told

133

you that I loved you ten years ago when I married you. I'll let you know if it changes.'

That would not be enough.

It sounds ridiculous, yet many managers behave like that towards their people. They are presumed to be doing a good job unless they are told otherwise.

That's not enough either. People are desperate for praise. They want to be noticed, recognized, valued and rewarded.

It is said that a dog will die for its master, a mother will die for her son, and a man will die ... if there's a big enough audience. Now we are not quite talking about dying, but you are asking people to involve themselves deeply in an organization, to give a large part of their lives to it, and to become committed to the organization's objectives. If you are asking so much of your people, they need a receptive audience – and you are that audience. If you are the boss, then you are sitting in the front row of the stalls and you had better be looking when they turn in a good performance.

Research into feedback yields paradoxical results. Most managers reckon to praise more often than they criticize, yet people reckon, on average, that they are criticized five times more often than they are praised. These ratios are probably similar for the relationship between parents and children. One explanation for this is that many managers offer praise and criticism together, and start with the praise: 'This is a very good report, but . . .' The recipient will only hear the word 'but'; the manager will think she has praised – in fact she will *know* that she has praised, but the person will not have heard the praise – therefore, the person will not have been praised.

There is also the curious phenomenon of the 'silent but', where the word is not spoken by the boss, but it is clearly heard. This problem stems, I suspect, from a reluctance to confront: some managers don't like giving bad news, so they soften people up with the good news, then slip in the criticism behind a 'but'. The effect is disastrous. Praise and recognition should be as specific as possible, and be given as close to the event as possible.

Sometimes, of course, it is necessary to give negative feedback. If someone is not achieving acceptable results then their boss must act. Tolerance of poor performance is a cancer which demotivates other people. Ultimately, if the person is not capable of learning to do the job well they may have to move to another job.

Reluctance to deal with poor performance is one of the greatest causes of inefficiency, and thus one of our greatest time-wasters.

Machiavelli put this point well. He said in effect: 'When you are doing good, do it little by little. Spread it out. Make it last a long time. When you are doing evil, get it over quickly.'

Praise frequently. It is a great motivator. Give negative feedback as rarely as possible, but when the need arises, do the job properly. Don't niggle and moan, that simply sours the atmosphere and the relationship. Call the person in and confront the problem, again specifically, as close to the event as possible and in a constructive manner. If possible finish the meeting with an item of good news so that the person does not go away blaming the whole incident on your foul mood.

THE MANAGER AS COACH

Training is a key high-leverage activity. In modern organizations, it is increasingly being seen as a line management responsibility. All managers have some responsibility for the training of their own staff, so experienced managers ought also to be experienced trainers, with years of practice behind them.

Unfortunately, this is not always the case. Many managers are poor at coaching, and because they don't do it well they tend to neglect it and devote themselves to easier activities. My starting point in looking at this subject is to change the focus from the trainer to the learner, and to suggest that you cannot *teach* anyone anything: the task is to help them to learn.

The most significant thing that can happen in a training session is that the learner might learn something. The factor which will have greatest impact in determining whether this learning takes place will be the state of mind of the *learner*. We all learn best when we want to learn – when we have a problem to solve or a skill we wish to acquire. We learn best when we are well motivated and when we feel reasonably confident, so the relationship between coach and trainee is vital. Do everything you can to raise their self-confidence.

Sometimes what goes on in so-called 'coaching sessions' ignores this. The coach decides what the learners should learn: the coach spends most of the time telling learners what they are doing wrong and how to do it right. In this critical atmosphere the learners can become defensive and demotivated and lose their self-confidence.

Why are some managers so quick to tell? I suspect it has something to do with showing off; with liking the sound of their own voices. Managers focus on the skill or knowledge they wish to transfer and forget about the person, the learner.

David Hemery, the Olympic gold medal hurdler and sports psychologist, devised a course based on the opposite extreme: 'Coaching through questioning'.

When I attended the course I found myself on a golf-driving range, attempting to coach a week-end golfer. Since I am not a golfer, I could not resort to telling. I started by asking the golfer what aspect of his game he would like to work on. 'My swing', he said, 'Sometimes I find I am tensing up as I swing.' I asked him where he felt this tension, whether it was in the shoulders, the arms, or the fingers. He didn't know.

I suggested he drive a few balls and notice the tension. I also suggested that he should not look to see where the balls had gone, that he should keep his head down and focus his entire attention on the process. After a few swings, he found it. 'It's in my hands. I am gripping the club too tightly,' he said. I asked him when he felt the tension. Was it before or after striking the ball? Again, he didn't know. After a few more practice swings he said, 'I've got it. It's just before I hit the ball. I think I am trying to re-adjust the swing as I am about to hit the ball.'

Already his drives were starting to go further and straighter. In just a few minutes as a coach I had helped this golfer to learn something but, far more importantly, I had raised his self-confidence and *empowered him to continue learning*. Telling blocks this awareness.

The sad thing about David Hemery's course was that some people found it very difficult. This applied particularly to some experienced school-teachers who were experts in the sport. They couldn't resist the temptation to tell. Even when they did ask questions, these tended to be manipulative, designed to bring out the point they wanted to make.

This is not to say that telling has no part to play in teaching. Telling is very simple and fast. Where the learner is a total novice, he or she will almost certainly need some basic instruction: the first-time golfer must be shown how to hold the club and how to swing.

Even the experienced learner who is confident and well-motivated may benefit from the occasional instruction.

But where confidence and motivation are weak, telling may be counter-productive. We frequently over-estimate the self-confidence of others, and must take every opportunity to boost it.

If your people want to learn, and if your aim is to help them to learn, then the time you spend coaching them ought to be the highlight of the week for them. Is it? Do they always look forward to their sessions with you? And if not, whose fault is that?

When you move from control to delegation and coaching, you no longer need to know all the answers (which is very exhausting), you just need some good questions:

- Who will take this on?
- How confident do you feel that you can complete it on time?
- What help do you need?

TIME-WASTERS

Showing off
Insecurity
RELUCTANCE TO CONFRONT
POOR COACHING SKILLS

17. Managing the Boss

'The Boss' usually comes high on the list of time-wasters, in one of the following forms.

- Some bosses give unclear objectives, and specialize in moving the goal posts without warning
- Other bosses don't tell you how you're doing
- Some do not give you enough authority. They stand over you, fussing and interfering, changing everything
- Others give too much authority, they disappear and leave everything to you
- Some don't listen
- And hardly any of them thank you

The bad news is that if you wish to succeed in an organization, you must do a good job and the criteria for doing a good job are set by your boss. If you work for someone else, you work to their priorities as they see them: that is the accountability structure of the organization. It isn't always comfortable, but it is a fact of life. That relationship must hold true if the organization is to operate efficiently. It is also known as the 'Golden Rule' of management. 'She who has the gold makes the rules.' (We'll continue to have a woman boss in this section: we need more of them.)

Does this mean that there is no hope? Does it mean you must wait until your boss attends a time management seminar? Of course not. There has to be something *you* can do.

When I attended my first management courses this puzzled me, because tutors only talked about managing subordinates, which I didn't find very difficult. They never talked about managing the boss, which seemed much harder.

I found the first part of my answer in a colleague's office one day. As I was sitting there interrupting him, the interruption was interrupted by a phone call. While waiting for him to finish the call I glanced through his desk calender, reading the sayings of the day, and there it was! A real beauty! It said: 'It's hell to work for a nervous boss, especially when it's you who's making her nervous.' I suddenly realized that was true – not just marginally true, but one of those deep and profound truths that is so obvious we overlook it.

If that is so true, then maybe part of the answer to managing your boss is to stop her feeling nervous, about you and your job performance.

Your boss is probably not equally nervous about all aspects of your work. There must be some areas where your boss is totally relaxed and confident in your abilities (ordering the stationery for example). In those areas, you get on with the job and don't bother her. Progress can be reported routinely at the end of the week or month.

There will inevitably be other areas where your boss has given you the authority to act, but does not seem totally confident. It is not in your interest for your boss to lose sleep over you, so never let her go to bed not knowing what you have done. Decide what needs to be done and do it – then tell your boss what you have done. That way you will keep her calm.

There will be other areas still where your boss has not given you the authority to act – never mind why for the moment – in those areas you should decide what needs to be done and take your recommendations to your boss.

If you are unlucky there may be yet another area of your job which gets your boss overexcited and makes her lose her cool occasionally. Never mention this part of the job, just sit tight and wait for her to tell you what to do.

This is the delegation scale again, but this time seen from below.

Within this framework, let's look at the specific problems listed earlier.

UNCLEAR OBJECTIVES AND MOVING GOAL POSTS

When I am invited into an organization as a consultant, to help people solve a problem, I often find that the reason they have failed to solve it for themselves is that they have been tackling the wrong problem, perhaps focusing on a symptom rather than the underlying causes. For that reason I would never accept a problem as originally stated. I would ask questions to find out about the background situation – the big picture – and when I have that I turn it into my words and feed it back: 'Let me see if I am understanding you correctly, you are saying that . . .' and in doing so I try to broaden it a little. At the end the other person either says 'Yes, that's it', or they give me more information. In due course we end up with a clearer definition of the project which we both understand.

With an external consultancy assignment the next stage is to put this project definition in writing, along with an outline plan for tackling it and a timescale. This helps to clarify the expectations of both parties and to ensure that they are compatible.

You can follow similar guidelines for internal assignments, even for quite small tasks. When your boss asks you to do something, you can say 'So what you are asking me to do is . . . I could get that done by Friday morning. Would that be OK?' For lengthy projects you could put it in writing the next day: 'Following our meeting yesterday I thought it might be useful for me to summarize what we agreed.'

- This is what I understand you asked me to do . . .
- I plan to tackle it in this way . . .
- My proposed timescale is . . .
- Please let me know if this is acceptable to you.

I suspect that one of the problems in the relationships between bosses and their people is that they are seen as parent/child relationships, with the parent telling the child what to do and the child having to obey.

Far healthier, especially in a modern 'flat' organization, is to think of the relationship as being between two adults, each of whom has different responsibilities within the organization. This makes it easier to see that both parties are responsible for ensuring that objectives are clear.

BOSSES WHO DON'T TELL YOU HOW YOU ARE DOING

We all need feedback, especially from our bosses and our customers, the people for whom we are working. Without feedback almost any job becomes drudgery. Imagine standing on a golf course all day, hitting golf balls but not seeing where they go. Even that would become very boring.

If you are not getting the feedback you need and want, *ask for it*, adult to adult. Do not spring this on your boss unexpectedly, give her time to prepare: 'I put a lot of effort into this report and I would very much like to hear your comments on my ideas and on the way I presented them. Could I come and see you later in the week?'

Don't be too quick to classify your boss as an adversary, remember that she is also dependent on you.

BOSSES WHO DON'T GIVE YOU ENOUGH AUTHORITY

The initial response to this problem is to ask for more authority – or rather to offer to take more responsibility. But if this doesn't work you might need another strategy.

How about the 'work to rule'? Where you have not been given the authority to act the rule is: 'Make recommendations.' Do just that. When something crops up in an area of your job in which you have insufficient authority, decide what needs to be done, then pop in to see your boss with your recommendations: 'This has just happened and here is what I propose to do.' Bosses like people who make recommendations.

The plan, however, is to be in and out of your boss's office as often as you can on such matters. Sooner or later there will come a day when she is under pressure: her desk is cluttered with work; her phone keeps ringing and she is trying to finish a report. When you walk in with your, 'This has just happened and here is what I propose to do,' she erupts: 'Do you have to keep coming in here and interrupting me? I thought you were learning something about time management.'

Instead of walking out cursing her under your breath, rush straight back to your desk and celebrate. You have just been promoted. In that split second she gave you permission to act without consulting her first. In that area of your job you have now moved up a level. Don't move straight to the top of the scale, find some intermediate point. Be careful to recognize, however, that in other areas of your job you will still be at the 'prepare it and I'll check it' stage. That was rather manipulative, wasn't it? But I assure you that the way to gain more responsibility is to make consistently good recommendations for a period of time. Some bosses grant the extra responsibility benignly at appraisal time, some when they are asked and some only when they are under pressure, but sooner or later you will get it, often followed nine months later by the salary that goes with it.

BOSSES WHO GIVE TOO MUCH AUTHORITY

You might think that the top of the scale – 'Do it your way' – is what you should be aiming for. In an ideal world that might be so, but in reality it can be highly dangerous. You may think that you have your boss's total confidence in some key area of your job. You may have been operating at the top of the scale for several months . . . then one day, when you are out of the office, a crisis emerges and, because you are not there, it lands on your boss's desk.

Suddenly she realizes that she doesn't know what you've been up to. When you return, you will be summoned to her office. You may be moved from the top of the scale to the bottom in ten seconds flat, and that can leave deep psychological scars. It is to be avoided.

At the top of the scale you are very exposed. It is therefore best suited to the low-risk, more routine aspects of your job. For the high-risk elements the furthest you should go is to do it your way, but tell your boss immediately what you have done. Even if she doesn't want to know, she can't stop you informing her, in writing if necessary. So this problem is entirely within your own control.

BOSSES WHO DON'T LISTEN

If your boss doesn't listen to you, try adopting a sales approach – develop your ideas and then sell them to your boss. As in all selling, the first step is to understand the customer's needs:

- What are the constraints and pressures on her?
- What is her preferred working style?
- What does she need to help her achieve her objectives? The best way to earn the gratitude of anyone is to help solve their problems

When you present your idea, lead in to it carefully:

'I've got an idea, would you like to hear it?'

'We were talking last week about the XYZ problem. Taking your idea further, I think . . .', etc.

It is also necessary to confront your boss occasionally with any problems that she is causing for you: frequent interruptions, unnecessary panics and so on. In such circumstances it is often a good idea to ask for advice. It may not be quite what you want but few people can resist the invitation.

Adopt a pro-active approach to your relationship. All the managers I meet agree that they would like their people to be more creative, to come up with more ideas. Take time out regularly to scan for opportunities, to look for ways to improve the efficiency and smooth running of your organization or to increase the satisfaction of its customers. Keep a steady trickle of ideas flowing towards your boss. You won't always be thanked for them, and your boss may steal some of them, but in the long run it must help your cause.

18. Working With Others

As well as dealing with people outside our own organization, most of whom can be classified as customers or suppliers, we have also to deal with other people inside the organization. In a modern organization these 'internal others' could also be thought of as customers and suppliers. The sales department is the customer of the production department which, in turn, is the customer of the purchasing department. Many people, like your secretary, will be both a supplier and a customer for you at different times. Good time management, or personal effectiveness, means understanding and managing these relationships.

In this chapter I shall use a marketing framework to analyse these relationships, drawing some simple lessons from the external marketplace which might be useful to you in dealing with your internal customers and internal suppliers.

The explosive growth of many free market economies, especially in comparison with centrally planned economies, has demonstrated the superiority of their relatively free market system. That is not to say that Western economies are totally free, nor that free-market economies do not create some worrying problems. But in *economic* terms, the free market works because the customer has a *choice*. Organizations compete for business by trying to understand and meet the needs of their customers, and this has been a major driving force for innovation, quality and cost-reduction.

If you want to find good quality products or good service, look in a competitive market, such as restaurants. If you want to find bad service, look at a monopoly. This is not to say that monopolies cannot provide good service – far from it – but it does seem easier to neglect innovation and quality in a captive market.

A question for operating managers: How many potential suppliers are competing for your custom when you require personnel services, or accounting services? Could this be a problem?

DELIVERING QUALITY TO CUSTOMERS

Delivering quality involves two key steps: discovering customers' needs, and meeting them. This, of course, is a simple definition of the marketing concept. It leads to a clear specification of customer requirements which the supplier must meet. But what about internal customers? Do you have clearly specified requirements for all your internal customers? Do you know exactly what they want from you? Or do they just get what you choose to supply?

DISCOVERING NEEDS

In the external market place this is called 'Market Research' or, more precisely, 'Qualitative Market Research'. Non-marketeers often think this means asking customers what they want. It should be far more than that, because customers tend not to innovate. Customers talk mostly in terms of the products and services with which they are familiar. Innovation is the suppliers' job.

This type of market research involves getting people talking, either in focus groups or individually; it involves working alongside them in their place of work, trying to understand the problems they

Imagine that your organization has four accounts departments. Whenever you need their services, you can choose between them on the basis of efficiency, customer care and value for money. What do you think will happen to the quality of their services?

are facing. Ultimately it should mean understanding your customers and their need for your services better than they understand it themselves.

How much time do you spend with your customers, internal or external, trying to understand them and their problems? How well do you understand their real needs? How often do you approach them with innovative solutions?

MARKET SEGMENTATION

Customer needs are different, so the question arises, 'How far should we go in providing different products or services to cater for these differing needs?' In the external marketplace marketing and sales managers tend to argue for greater differentiation and segmentation in order to meet customer needs. From the other side, the controllers of this world tend to argue for greater standardization, because they see that as the foundation of efficiency.

In his book *The Competitive Advantage of Nations*, Michael Porter points out that most countries which are rich in natural resources, such as Australia, Canada and Brazil, have been surprisingly unsuccessful economically because they tend to focus on tons and cost-control. In contrast, among the most successful economies we find Japan, Singapore and Switzerland – all of them notable for their lack of natural resources. These countries have had to focus on adding value, and they have done that by understanding customer needs and differentiating.

The external market place has shown that, if the quality is real in the eyes of the customer, then they will pay for it. Unfortunately, in the internal market place, cost control too often wins the day and monopoly suppliers force their standard systems and services on every customer.

Could you improve the perceived quality of your products or services through greater differentiation?

MEETING CUSTOMERS' NEEDS

Having discovered and specified the needs, the supplier must meet those needs or, better still, exceed them. The external market place has taught us that the way to create happy customers is to under-promise and over-deliver.

It simply isn't good enough to meet customer needs nine times out of ten: if you call at your bank once a week and get good service nine times and bad service once, what will you talk about with your friends? Quality is ten times out of ten: on time, on specification, every time.

Quality is, in part, subjective. Where an organisation has a good image, like Marks and Spencer, loyal customers will overlook an occasional lapse. Where organizations have a bad image, like railways in Britain, people delight in swapping stories about their failures, and the problem is compounded.

In the same way that your company has an image in the minds of your customers and suppliers, so does your unit. It has been built up through time from their experiences in dealing with you and it will have a major impact on their perception of quality. Try to look at your unit from the point of view of one of your internal customers, and scrutinize your image:

- Do you always do what you have promised, at the time that you promised, without having to be reminded?
- Are you always on time?
- What is the first impression I would get if I were to enter your office?
- What is the first impression I would get if I were to telephone you?
- Do you always deliver quality?
- Do you make it easy for people to deal with you.

MEASUREMENT

In the external market place we have learned the value of measurement. People pay attention to the things that are measured, but it is no longer sufficient to measure volume and profit – we must get feedback from customers to enable us to measure quality and customer satisfaction. Do you get regular feedback from your internal customers?

CUSTOMER COMPLAINTS

The complaints received by any organization are only ever the tip of the iceberg. Most customers don't complain, they just swap stories with other customers. That being so, I suggest that any organization is lucky when a customer complains: the customer is providing important information which can help the organization improve its quality. Therefore all organizations should welcome complaints and should make it as easy as possible for customers to complain.

How easy do you make it for your customers to complain? How good are you at welcoming complaints?

Dealing with monopoly suppliers

While running a seminar in Nairobi, I heard a complaint from a Colgate Palmolive manager about the appalling service provided by a local hotel for a major promotional function. The manager finished his story by saying, 'We have used that hotel for all our visitors and functions for 12 years, but we will never ever use it again.' I was rather surprised because I had worked with some of the middle managers of the hotel concerned and thought they were trying hard and providing good service, so I went to see them. When I had passed on the story, I received this interesting response: 'I know exactly who caused that problem. He joined us six months ago and has been causing problems ever since. We have tried to teach him our methods and failed. Now we are trying to get rid of him. Please go back to Colgate Palmolive and get them to complain at the highest possible level and as loudly as they can. That is the only way we can solve this problem.'

In every organization there will be people who are trying to give good service. If we don't complain, we are not helping them. Indeed it has often been suggested that service standards in the UK are poor because we don't complain enough.

Make sure your monopoly suppliers know exactly what your needs are, and give them regular feedback on your satisfaction. Anyone genuinely wishing to give good service will always welcome this dialogue – and it must be the route to innovation.

ANOTHER DIMENSION TO INTERNAL MARKETING

Maybe we should see all employees as customers for the services provided by the organization and its managers.

In the external market place, marketing is necessary because the customers have a choice. Increasingly, employees have a choice: they can join your organization, or not; they can turn up for work, or not; and they can bring energy and commitment, or not.

(For a detailed exploration of this approach, see Kevin Thomson's book *The Employee Revolution*.)

PRIORITIZING PEOPLE

Dialogues with customers and suppliers, listening skills, building and maintaining relationships . . . all of these take time, and time is in short supply. How can we prioritize people?

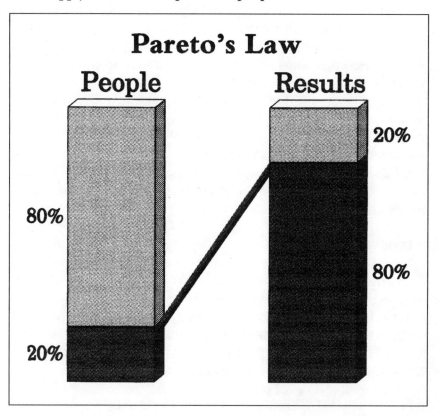

Applying Pareto's law to this problem would suggest that 20 per cent of the people you have dealings with probably influence 80 per cent of your results, and 80 per cent of the people influence 20 per cent of the results. If this is so, then you must decide who falls in which category, and treat them accordingly. Draw up a list of your high-leverage relationships as follows:

- Your boss – she is the major source of your priorities
- Two or three people at or above your boss's level who have the greatest influence on her
- Everyone who reports directly to you
- Anyone else within your organization whose support you must have to do your job effectively. If the list starts to look too long at this stage, ask yourself whether you could delegate any of these relationships to a member of your team
- Other people outside your organization, but again only the essential ones. In terms of customers and suppliers, that means finding some way to distinguish between key contacts and other contacts. This is always a very difficult line to draw. Every customer must have someone within the organization who will look after their interests, but it cannot always be you

Effective managers build networks of relationships among their key contacts, both internal and external. They spend time with these people, getting to know them as individuals and learning to trust one another. This can be a very high-leverage activity in the long run. They know that they cannot achieve anything significant without the help of others but they also know that they don't have time for everybody.

TIME-WASTERS

Reluctance to confront
Poor coaching skills
POOR UNDERSTANDING OF CUSTOMER NEEDS
OVER-STANDARDIZATION OF SERVICE
INSUFFICIENT FEEDBACK FROM CUSTOMERS
WEAK RELATIONSHIPS WITH KEY PEOPLE
LACK OF INNOVATION

PART III
WHY DO WE DO IT?

Here is Edward Bear coming downstairs now, bump, bump, bump, on the back of his head, behind Christopher Robin. It is, as far as he knows, the only way of coming downstairs, but sometimes he feels that there really is another way if only he could stop bumping for a moment and think of it.

Winnie the Pooh:
A.A. Milne,

Isn't that what so many of us are doing? We rush around making the same mistakes day after day, falling into the same traps, putting increasing pressure on ourselves and dreaming of the sun, the sea and a beautiful sandy beach where we could . . . stop.

Why do we do it? The problems have been around for many years, the answers have been known, so why are so many managers still trapped?

This section is more philosophical in nature. It seeks to explore that question: why do we do it?

19. Why Do We Do It?

You have a report to write for the board meeting. When you originally agreed to write it, a couple of weeks ago, you were quite excited. It is a real opportunity to influence a significant decision and to demonstrate your own ability. Time is now running out: the task has finally reached the top of your list of priorities, but the meeting is tomorrow.

You are about to start work on it when the phone rings. It is a customer with a serious problem; then there is a production breakdown; then a colleague falls ill. All in all, it's one of those days.

Suddenly people start going home. Surely it can't be 5 o'clock already? But it is. You realize with horror that you are not going to write that report this afternoon. Never mind, you will have to do it at home: not ideal, but you have done it before; you still have time.

When you get home, you feel exhausted and tense. It has been a bad day. A quick drink will help you relax. When you have finished dinner you decide to watch the news before starting work – after all, it is important to keep up to date with events in the world at large. The programme after the news is really very interesting as well, and you are too tired now. You will have an early night and write the report at 6.00a.m.

Somehow or other it is 7.00a.m. before you get up. You grab a piece of toast and rush off to work. The report does get produced, but with no time to check it, before the 10 o'clock meeting. It is a pale shadow of what you envisaged two weeks ago.

This syndrome is neatly encapsulated in a book called *The Last Minute Manager* – the story of a manager who makes all the mistakes. It includes this marvellous description: 'The Last Minute Manager aims high, and almost always nearly makes it.' I don't know about you, but I felt ill when I read that. It was so recognizable. Why do we do it?

In order to answer this question we must analyse the problem in greater depth. The most common mistake in problem-solving is to concentrate on the symptoms and fail to see the underlying causes. Good problem-solving means systematically tracing each problem to its ultimate cause, and then solving that underlying problem so that it never occurs again. I suggest you take a few of your most significant time-wasters and try the exercise. Since most of these underlying causes are in the mind, this exercise is highly personal. I cannot answer for you. However, I have produced a few samples to stimulate your thinking.

In analysing some of your problems you may be tempted to ascribe their cause to someone else. This is a futile exercise, in part because it puts you in a 'loser' frame of mind ('It's not my fault') and in part because it reduces the chances of changing anything. What are the chances of success for New Year resolutions imposed by wives on their husbands (or vice versa)?

If you still believe that the principal cause of a problem lies elsewhere (and occasionally the external world does conspire to trip us up) then the analysis should be 'In what way have I contributed to this?' Here are some examples of problem analysis:

1. Problem: I have lost an important document. Why?
Answer: Because my desk is untidy.

For this problem, the superficial solution would be to tidy the desk but, as suggested earlier, spring-cleaning of this sort is largely a waste of time because it has only dealt with the symptom. In order to discover the underlying problem the analysis must continue, as follows:

New Problem: Why is my desk untidy?
Answer: Because I don't have a good filing system.
New Problem: Why don't I have a good filing system?
Answer: Because I haven't designed one.
New Problem: Why haven't I designed a good filing system?
Answer: Because I have been too busy.
New Problem: Why have I been too busy to design a good filing system?
Answer: Because I tend to do the urgent and the easy before the high-leverage tasks.

The deeper solution is to develop a better system of prioritizing, and to set as one priority task the development of a new filing system.

2. Problem: I am sometimes late for appointments. Why?

I schedule my time too tightly, leaving no margin for error. Why?

I try to be efficient and avoid wasting time.

Possible Solution: Recognize the cost and embarrassment of your occasional lateness. Aim to get to all future appointments earlier, and take some simple work with you to avoid wasting time.

3. Problem: I am overloaded, I have far too much to do. Why?

I have trouble saying 'No'. Why?

I want to be liked. Why?

I am afraid of being rejected. Why?

I am lacking in self-confidence.

Possible Solution: Reflect on your strengths and skills. What are the things you are good at? What have you done well in the past? People may prefer you to be efficient and cheerful rather than overloaded and depressed. Practise saying 'No' firmly, but without offending.

4. Problem: My relationship with my family is deteriorating. Why?

I get irritable. Why?

I feel I should be catching up on my paperwork.

Possible Solution: Either ignore the work and concentrate on the family or, if you must, ignore the family and concentrate on the work. Devoting your time to the family and your emotional energy to feeling guilty gives everyone the worst of both worlds. Try this method of problem analysis with some of your own time-wasters.

TIME-WASTERS

Insufficient feedback from customers
Weak relationships with key people
LACK OF PLANNING
POOR SYSTEMS
OVER-TIGHT SCHEDULES
LACK OF SELF-CONFIDENCE
FEELING GUILTY
The time has come to review our master list of time-wasters, which could be a painful process. I remind you that there is no suggestion that *everybody* suffers from *all* these problems – far from it – but each

of us is likely to have a number of weaknesses, some of which will have been captured here.

TIME-WASTERS

INTERRUPTIONS
MEETINGS
TELEPHONE
CRISES AND PANICS
THE BOSS
FAULTY EQUIPMENT
CHASING PEOPLE
LACK OF RESOURCES
JUNK MAIL
READING
FORM FILLING
TRAVEL
SOCIAL CHAT
LACK OF SKILL OR KNOWLEDGE
CREATING CRISES
LEAVING THINGS UNTIL THE LAST MINUTE
FIREFIGHTING IS FUN
NEGLECT OF FIRE PREVENTION
POST-ADRENALIN DIP
COMFORTABLE, FAMILIAR, EASY JOBS
IMMEDIATE REWARD
PROCRASTINATION
CLUTTERED DESK
SPRING-CLEANING THE DESK
POOR FILING SYSTEM
LACK OF RELIABLE LISTS
NOT FINISHING THINGS
ENJOYING INTERRUPTIONS
ALLOWING UNNECESSARY INTERRUPTIONS
OPEN-PLAN OFFICES
READING LOW-VALUE MATERIAL
POOR READING SKILLS
LACK OF CONCENTRATION
FORGETTING

FAILURE TO LEARN AND REMEMBER
WORKING LONG HOURS
BEING TIRED
LAZINESS
POOR SENSE OF TIME
INABILITY TO SAY NO
OVER-LENGTHY REPORTS
BORING PRESENTATIONS
TALKING TOO MUCH
RELUCTANCE TO ASK SIMPLE QUESTIONS
PRETENDING TO KNOW
NOT LISTENING
PREMATURE EVALUATION
RESISTANCE TO FEEDBACK
POOR RAPPORT SKILLS
LACK OF CONFIDENCE IN PEOPLE
NEED TO FEEL IN CONTROL
FAILURE TO DEVELOP PEOPLE
UNCLEAR BOUNDARIES
IDENTITY CRISIS
NEED TO BE LIKED
MY PEOPLE ARE HAVING TROUBLE WITH THEIR BOSS
SHOWING OFF
INSECURITY
RELUCTANCE TO CONFRONT
POOR COACHING SKILLS
POOR UNDERSTANDING OF CUSTOMER NEEDS
INSUFFICIENT FEEDBACK FROM CUSTOMERS
WEAK RELATIONSHIPS WITH KEY PEOPLE
LACK OF INNOVATION
LACK OF PLANNING
POOR SYSTEMS
OVER-STANDARDIZATION OF SERVICES
OVER-TIGHT SCHEDULES
LACK OF SELF-CONFIDENCE
FEELING GUILTY

We do the little jobs before the big ones.
We do what we enjoy before what we find less pleasant.

We do the easy before the hard.

We do the familiar before the new.

We deal with the interrupters before the priorities.

We deal with the urgent before the important.

We tackle the job on top of the pile before the one that is lower down.

We tackle the short term before the long term.

And above all, we do what we have been asked to do, by our boss, by our customers, by our colleagues – and even by complete strangers – before we follow our own priorities.

At our worst, we operate without a strategy and without clear objectives. We operate with inadequate systems and plans. We drift through the day, blown about by events and letting time slip through our fingers.

Why do we do it? How can it be that so many otherwise intelligent people lose control of their time and end up chasing, patching, coping and just getting by? Lack of time seems to be the most common complaint in modern society, yet most people do little about it. Why?

This question fascinates me.

20. *Are You a Pigeon or a Person?*

I suspect that our mistake is in thinking of ourselves as rational beings, when rationality accounts for only part of our behaviour. Have you ever had one drink too many in the evening? Sometimes when you can be fairly sure you will regret it in the morning? Or a large helping of Black Forest gateau, with extra cream? In many situations, our attitudes and beliefs say one thing, but we do another.

Where do those 'non-rational' aspects of our behaviour come from? Probably from our animal instincts.

THE EVOLUTION OF THE BRAIN

The evolution of the brain has occurred in stages, in parallel with our physical evolution from our primitive mammalian ancestors.

Automatic reflexes like the knee jerk are controlled by the lowest level, at the top of the spinal cord. The cerebellum, on top of that, controls movement and monitors the senses; the hypothalamus controls hunger, thirst, shivering and influences sleep, sexual drives and emotions. The neo-cortex, the most recent addition to the brain, deals with the higher-level processes including consciousness and speech.

Many of our drives and instincts are still those of the animal. At that animal level we are attracted to things we find rewarding and pleasant, and repelled by things we find painful or unpleasant. To the extent that we operate at this animal level, our behaviour is there-fore conditioned by rewards and punishments.

The best-known early studies of conditioned behaviour in animals were those of Pavlov and his dogs. His work was taken up and extended by the American psychologist Skinner.

In one experiment, Skinner trained a pigeon to turn a complete circle in a clockwise direction. Every time the bird turned to the right, it was given a grain of corn. Eventually it 'recognized' this pattern and would turn to the right and peck the corn, turn and peck. The experimenter then stretched the distance the bird had to move to get the grain of corn, until eventually the bird was turning in complete circles.

To take a bird with no prior experience and 'train' it to turn complete circles would take less than 15 minutes. What is it that makes the bird turn? Clearly, the answer is: REWARD. Skinner's theory can be stated in six words: 'Behaviour that is rewarded is repeated.'

Picture a school classroom. The time is 9.00a.m. The teacher is ready to start the lesson, but there is a lot of noise. Suddenly he shouts: 'QUIET!' What happens? It goes quiet. What will he do the next time he is faced with the same situation? The same again. 'Behaviour that is rewarded is repeated.' And he tends not to notice that he has to shout just a little louder and a little more often as the months go by. So the pupils condition the teacher.

Since this conditioning operates at the animal level the rewards

Are you a pigeon or a person?

that drive it are the immediate rewards. It is the immediate satisfaction of silence *now* that blinds the teacher to the long-term consequences.

It is the pleasure of another drink *now* that outweighs the risk of a hangover tomorrow. Like the pigeon in the cage, we spin round for a few grains of corn. It is the taste of that cream gateau *now* – I can always diet tomorrow.

I am not suggesting that human behaviour is all driven from this animal level. I don't agree with Skinner's views that conditioning is the answer to every problem. Between stimulus and response we have freedom of choice. We are moral and ethical beings with consciences and we have brains which apply logic and can develop long-term strategies. I am simply suggesting that we can sometimes get seduced by immediate reward, and thereby undermine our higher plans by doing the easy and pleasant tasks, oblivious to our own long-term interests.

Look again at the list of timewasters in chapter 19. Most of them involve doing things that yield some immediate reward, but at the cost of a longer term objective.

The marshmallow test

In a famous experiment, children were offered one marshmallow now, which was put on a plate in front of them, or two marshmallows when the experimenter returned, after about ten minutes. The experimenter would then leave the room.

Those children who delayed gratification and waited for the double benefit tended to be more successful in their later careers – and the marshmallow test turned out to be a more accurate predictor of career success than IQ measurement or any other tests.

Are you strong enough, as a person, to determine your own objectives and pursue them, or do you run round in circles for immediate gratification?

21. The Greatest Time-Waster of Them All

The previous chapter painted a somewhat cynical and unflattering view of humanity. How can the Last Minute Managers of this world live with the results of their behaviour? How can they tolerate the constant stress? How is it that they cannot see what they are doing?

I believe that we survive by externalizing our problems, by blaming them on someone else. 'Post event rationalization' is, to me, the greatest time-waster of them all because it is the means by which we conceal our true problems from ourselves.

This has been best illustrated by Leon Festinger in his work on 'Cognitive Dissonance'. Festinger travelled around the United States, purportedly advizing record manufacturers how many copies of each record to produce. He invited teenage schoolgirls to assist in his 'research'. They were asked to listen to ten brand new pop records and to rate them so that he could advise the company how many copies to produce. That was not true, but it was what each girl was told. When a girl had rated all ten records she was thanked for her help and offered, as a reward, a copy of one of the new records. In each case the girl would be allowed to choose between two of the records. She would choose one to keep, thus simultaneously rejecting the chance to keep the other.

Just as she was leaving, an assistant in a white coat would rush into the room and say: 'I'm very sorry, but the machine on which you recorded your scores was not working properly and they have all been erased. Please could you come back into the sound booth and rate them again?'

When the girl had completed the second set of ratings, the experimenters would compare them with her first ratings. They discovered an interesting phenomenon. Eight of the ten records would have roughly the same score. There were slight variations, but they had no statistical significance. However, in a significant number of cases the record that the girl had chosen to keep got a slightly higher score on the second list than on the first. And the record she had chosen to reject got a slightly lower score. What seems to be happening here is that the behaviour, the choice of the record, is influencing the girl's attitude.

Let's put that into a familiar context: suppose that I am about to buy a car: I survey the market place with dozens of makes and hundreds of models; I render this down to a short-list; then I compare, I test drive and I choose.

For the sake of simplicity, let us suppose that I have reduced my short-list to two. Either I shall buy a sports car, which would be great fun to drive, would impress my clients and would smarten my image; or I shall buy a large estate car, which might be rather boring to look at, but would have much more space for my children.

These two cars may be very different, but I am having trouble choosing between them. Each, in its own way, is equally attractive. However, I do have to take a decision, so I eventually buy the estate car.

Two months later, I am sitting in the bar at Ashridge, minding my own business, when a colleague walks in. He has a new car. It happens to be the sports car I nearly bought, and he starts to tell me how it has brought back the joy to driving, how it is impressing the clients, and on and on he goes.

What is running through my mind? I translate his remarks and hear him saying: 'You are stupid. You bought the wrong car.' I don't like that message. I don't like to think that I take bad decisions, and when I have backed that decision with many thousand pounds of my own money, I very much don't like what I am hearing. This is an example of cognitive dissonance.

How can I avoid this nasty feeling? Well, the easy option is to walk away and avoid my colleague for the next few months. But that doesn't really resolve the problem. I could tell him about the advantages of my car, but they would hardly be likely to impress him, and in any case I nearly bought that sports car two months ago.

Can I now persuade myself that the car I chose is better and the one I rejected worse than it was then?

What I do, and what I suspect we all do under these circumstances is this: as I listen to my colleague eulogising his new car, I say to myself: 'What a fool. A new toy, that's what he's bought. A status symbol. I'm glad I'm not like him. What matters to me is comfort and safety. I'm a family man.'

I cannot change the car, but I *can change myself*. My self-image and attitudes shift to justify my earlier behaviour. Research has shown that attitudes can change much more dramatically after purchase than before. We often buy for emotional or psychological reasons — but then justify our behaviour using logic.

If there was a full-page colour advertisement for a BMW in today's newspaper, there is one category of reader who could be almost guaranteed to read it – no, not the people who are thinking of buying a BMW, but the people *who recently bought one*. Similarly when you have recently bought a house, the property pages of the local newspaper are of burning interest as you compare current prices with what *you* paid. These advertisements would meet a very powerful need – the need for *reassurance*. We all have a great need to bolster our own ego and belief in our own judgment.

We also have a tremendous ability to externalize our problems and blame them on someone else. It saves us having to face up to our own shortcomings. The Last Minute Manager blames his problems on the interrupters, on his boss, and on the industry he works in; the late arrival at the meeting blames the traffic; the unsuccessful sales-person blames the customer or the pricing policy; the manager blames her subordinates.

Think of a specific time, not too far back, when you felt bad about work. It may only have lasted for ten minutes, or it may have lasted longer. Relive the occasion for a few moments. Here are some questions to help you:

- When did it happen?
- What triggered the feeling?
- How did you feel?
- How long did it last?
- Who else was associated with those feelings?

And one more question: At that time, when you were feeling bad about work, did any of the following thoughts pass through your mind?

- This is a terrible organization to work for
- I didn't choose him as my boss
- It's not my day today
- It's not my fault
- I can't supervise everything

When we win, we are proud to stand tall and take the credit: 'That was me. I am a good manager. I did that!' When we lose, it hurts! We have a remarkable tendency to avoid the pain of failure by seeing ourselves as innocent victims and blaming the rest of the world. This is a natural human reaction. We do not like to fail and we can avoid much of the pain of failure by blaming it on other people. The excuses above are the words of the losers of this world, the people who are going nowhere. Listen to the conversations around you and all too often, you will hear things like: 'It's just my luck', 'It's society', 'It always rains on my holiday', 'It's the government' – and above all, the refrain, 'It's not my fault'.

Now that is very convenient, because if it's not my fault, then there is no need for me to do anything about it. So I don't. So I am back there again tomorrow in the same position.

While this might make for a less uncomfortable life in the short term, it does have considerable disadvantages in the longer term. We must learn to strip away the excuses and confront the real issues.

THE BAD NEWS is that there is nobody to blame but yourself.

THE GOOD NEWS is that the problems are treatable. You have plenty of options.

Some people give in to the chaos. They drift along with cluttered desks, cluttered diaries and cluttered lives, reacting to whatever happens and complaining when things go wrong. Others get organized. They are always on time, up to date and relaxed.

We all know people who have mastered time: the career woman who doubles as wife and mother and still finds time to entertain; the senior executive who can always spare half an hour if you need to talk; the colleague with six active hobbies.

Opinion polls show that managers complain about lack of time more often than anything else, unaware that the problem is *in the mind*. Those who cast themselves in the role of victim will be proved right – it is a self-fulfilling prophecy. They will be comforted by the knowledge that the world is unfair and that it was not their fault. Those who cast themselves as heroes or heroines have a chance.

22. Habits

Another explanation of our apparently illogical behaviour is that we human beings are creatures of habit: we do today what we did yesterday; we 'think' today what we 'thought' yesterday; for much of the time we don't really think at all.

Habits are the building blocks of life. We couldn't possibly live in the way we do without them. When you are getting dressed in the morning, you don't think 'Now I must take the button hole in one hand, placing my thumb over the hole, grasp the button between the thumb and first finger of my other hand, bring them together and . . .' you just do it without thinking. Could you describe the way you tie a shoelace, detailing which finger you use for each movement, without touching a shoelace?

Cast your mind back to the first time you tried to drive a car. You discovered that you had to put your left foot on the clutch and your right foot on the accelerator, while moving the gear lever with one hand, and holding the steering wheel in the other hand, and looking through the windscreen to see where you were going, and steering the car, and watching the mirror – and all while the person beside you was talking. It was quite a frightening experience. You may well have thought you would never be able to cope with it all.

Now, if you drive regularly, do you think about your left hand or your right foot? Never! In fact you can sometimes cover a considerable distance while using the brain to daydream, or to carry out a lengthy interactive conversation. Habits allow us to accomplish complex tasks, while freeing the mind to think about something else.

They are, therefore, invaluable and essential to our daily lives. The problem is that habits always take us to the same place. Five days a week I leave home at 7.00a.m. to drive to work. Sometimes on a Saturday I leave home at 7.30a.m. and set off down the same road in an attempt to get to the market in Berkhamsted. This involves turning left off my weekday route. I find that extraordinarily difficult. Time and again I drive straight past the turning. As habits operate at the subconscious level, it can be very hard to break them.

That is what much of this book has been about, habits, patterns of behaviour and skills, breaking old ones and forming new ones. It is not easy, but if you are going to change the way you behave, this is the problem you face. I would like to take you through one more example before describing a formula which I have found most useful.

I used to play a lot of squash, often with managers who came on courses. One day I found myself on court with someone who turned out to be a member of the Kenyan national squash team. I did not play squash to that standard! After a few minutes, he offered to give me some advice. That's good! I like learning, though I don't always like being taught.

The first thing he said was: 'Martin, you tower over the ball and you never bend your knees. You can't play decent squash unless you bend your knees.' So he demonstrated and I practised, then we started again.

As I approached the ball, he shouted 'KNEES'.

What do you think happened to my squash? It deteriorated sharply.

After a few minutes he stopped me again and said 'Martin, you are holding the racket dangling from your wrist. Keep your wrist firm, with the racquet head above the level of your hand . . . like this, down into the shot, wrist below the level of the ball.'

So off we went again. I concentrated hard on my wrist and he shouted 'KNEES!', then I thought about my knees and he said 'WRIST'. By this time it was almost impossible to hit the ball at all.

However he was nothing if not persistent, and a few moments later he said 'Martin, on the backhand, your backswing . . .' 'HOLD IT! HOLD IT!' I said, 'I cannot possibly take any more feedback.'

That is the problem you face now. There may be several changes of habit which you would like to make. They are not going to be easy. My strong advice is *not to try to change too much at once*. The following is a four stage process for developing a new skill or habit.

- Stage one is called *Unconscious Incompetence*, otherwise known as blissful ignorance.

- Then a helpful expert comes along and tells you what you are doing wrong. This stage is called *Conscious Incompetence* because nothing has changed yet. You may feel less happy than you did before, because you are aware of what you are doing wrong.
- Stage three is *Conscious Competence*, and it is exceedingly painful. You are doing it right, but you are only doing it that way because you have been told to. Anyone who has ever tried to change the way they hold a golf club, tie a necktie or make a speech knows how it feels, and the result is almost invariably counter-productive . . . to start with.
- But the only way to acquire any skill is to practise doing it right until you can do it without having to think about it, which is stage four – *Unconscious Competence*.

Nobody can learn a complex skill in a day, least of all from a book. The only way to learn that skill, whether it is playing golf, public speaking or time management, is to take one aspect of the skill, practise doing it right until it becomes easy and comfortable, and then move on to the next element in the skill.

The trouble is that we give up too easily when it becomes uncomfortable, especially if we don't see any immediate improvement in results. Since much of what we do regularly is made easy and smooth by habits and patterns, any change will be difficult until we develop new habits. All things are difficult before they become easy. Watching a learner playing golf, driving a car or putting up wallpaper is a frustrating experience. Learners make it difficult. Every movement is deliberate and stiff. The same must be true for those who are learning to manage, to delegate or to sell.

Any improvement implies change and change is always de-skilling and discomforting – so much so we are often tempted to stay in our old ruts, however uncomfortable they are.

But the end result of learning a skill is mastery. The true professional in any field makes it look easy. Watching a really skilful salesperson leading a customer through a conversation, sensitive not only to what the person is saying but to the intonations, the choice of words and images, posture, breathing patterns, changes of skin tone and any other signs of emotion, is astonishing. How on earth can the salesperson process so much complex information at the same time?

The answer is that it is easy. It's just like driving a car. Nobody is born like this. The salesperson has developed this skill over many years. Michelangelo is reputed to have said 'If people knew how hard I worked to attain my mastery, it wouldn't seem so wonderful after all.'

We have to work at the skills involved. Like all skills, they can be learned, and mastering them will move us from tension and stress to serenity and effectiveness.

Think of the pleasure you take in using the skills that you have. If you are good at cooking, karaoke singing, playing tennis, selling or running parties you will enjoy using those skills. Any skill can be developed to the point where it will bring you pleasure. For some people, the thought of talking to a group of 36 managers for three hours would induce paralysis. As a natural introvert I once felt exactly the same, but it is my job and I have worked hard at it.

Making a start is difficult and uncomfortable. There may be a considerable period of conscious competence, but gradually you will find it becomes easier and pleasanter. You will enlarge your comfort zones and develop new and more productive hobbies and habits.

Learning can be one of our greatest motivators. Developing and practising a new skill can be immensely satisfying, and the feeling of

Life is easier for the expert

control that it engenders does wonders for self-esteem. Those who have stopped learning become boring and cynical.

To summarize the process for changing a habit:

- Decide what change you want to make and make that change immediately
- Don't try to change too much at one time. Master the first change before embarking on the second
- Set yourself clear and measurable performance standards for your new behaviour
- Never, ever allow exceptions
- And don't expect an immediate improvement in results. It may take time and practice

PART IV
PLANNING FOR
SUCCESS

Successful organizations have clear objectives. The owner or senior managers find time to determine these objectives and occasionally to review and revise them. The corporate objectives are then transmitted around the organization so that everybody knows what it stands for and what they should be trying to achieve. This gives the successful organization a coherent value system which steers the decisions and actions of its managers. It is difficult to see how an organization could succeed without clear objectives, indeed it would be difficult to assess *whether* it had succeeded without knowing what it was trying to achieve.

Having determined their objectives, the good management team galvanizes the members of the organization to decide how they will achieve those objectives. They draw up plans, forecasts and budgets so that people will know exactly what is expected of them.

Finally, at the end of each month or week, actual performance is compared with the plan so that remedial action can be taken where needed.

I believe that the same process is necessary for each of us as individuals. We need objectives to give us direction, we need plans if we are to achieve those objectives, and we must review progress regularly against those plans. This is the subject of the final section of the book.

23. Goal Setting and Values

THE IMPORTANCE OF CLEAR GOALS

Where do you want to go in your life? Few people ever get round to answering that question in any but the vaguest of terms, but if you don't know where you want to go, you will probably end up somewhere else.

We cannot master time unless we know where we are going. Goals give meaning to time and provide a framework for the choices we must make; without clear goals, time management is pointless. These goals must come from within. The questions are easy to ask, but much harder to answer.

If I were to command you to be happy for as long as you live, what would you do? Many people think of a blue sky, warm sun, the sea and sand as their earthly paradise . . . but for how long? Even an idyllic island could become a prison.

Every day many people with no deep purpose complete a lot of goals: they write letters, fill in forms, answer the phone and tick things off on their 'to do' lists. In the short run they feel good; they can see progress: but without a deeper purpose this 'busyness' and routine can also imprison. Ask an older person for their regrets and they will usually talk about the things they didn't do.

Do you know anyone who is bored, tired and lacking in energy? Ask them for their objectives – the chances are that they won't have any realistic ones. Lack of purpose is a major cause of depression. Such people avoid creating a vision to protect themselves from disappointment and failure; they have opted for the security and familiarity of the status quo, because setting and pursuing objectives means leaving a comfort zone.

There are three sorts of people: those who make things happen, those who watch things happen and those who wonder what happened. Which of these categories are you choosing for yourself?

Objectives make us accountable to ourselves; they provide a benchmark for evaluating our actions; setting and pursuing objectives means taking a chance and applying some energy. If these objectives make work and life more meaningful, they will create motivation and generate energy. The route to fulfilment is rarely comfortable and the first step must be devoted to setting objectives.

For most of us there is more to life than work. Occasionally, I meet people who have decided to devote themselves solely to work and who, like calendar calculators have narrowed their focus to develop only a small fraction of their human potential. For them, a major promotion accompanied by a broken marriage and ulcers seems to be defined as success. Sometimes a major life crisis is needed to help such people realize that there is more to life than work. Others learn earlier that a happy life is a balanced life, so I shall look at goal-setting under four headings: personal, family, career and community.

PERSONAL GOALS

Do you want to be thinner or fitter, to read faster, to speak a second language or play better squash? Is there a hobby you would like to take up one day? Many of us dream of such things. We carry these dreams with us through our lives but never do anything about them.

Me? I want to improve my French. I've been saying that for years, but I've never done anything about it.

Our lives are full of books we have never read, records we have listened to once and expensive audio equipment used only for background music. Add to that the video cassettes recorded but never watched, the bicycles and rowing machines gathering dust – it's firefighting and busyness again, recreating our working styles at home.

Some people neglect personal goals, seeing them as self-indulgent, and choosing to devote themselves to serving others. I disagree. I see self-growth as a most important goal.

Many of the problems mentioned in this book have stemmed, at root, from lack of self-confidence. It is only when we start to develop our full potential as human beings that we become strong enough to offer healthy love to our families, that we gain the confidence to say 'I don't know' and that we grow to become good teachers, managers and parents. Then we are much more capable of helping others. Do not expect others to make you happy – that is your job. Treat yourself to a couple of personal goals, and some time to work on them.

FAMILY GOALS

All managers should ask themselves regularly: 'Do I have the right balance between work and family? Do I do enough for the people who love me, need me and depend on me? Do I give them enough of my time and enough of my energy, or do they just get the remains at the end of the day when there is nothing better to do?'

I am appalled by the frequency with which managers, when invited to set objectives, start with 'I want to spend more time with my family.' If that could be you, then for goodness sake don't let that remain a dream. Families are not for ever: children grow up with amazing speed; marriages can break up. We all need to be reminded regularly that you cannot do a kindness too soon, because you never know how soon it might be too late.

A young mother was tucking her small daughter up in bed the day before Grandma was coming to stay. 'We're going to have a visitor tomorrow – someone you know very well.'

The little girl looked up eagerly and said, 'Is it Daddy?'

If that hurts, do something about it.

- What could you do to strengthen the bonds of love that bind you to your family?
- What could you do to build the self-confidence of every member of your family?
- Could you set some specific goals for yourself in relation to each member of your family?

CAREER GOALS

How far will you go in your career? Will you get to the 'top'? Many people doubt whether they have the intelligence to get to the top but I can tell you, having worked with a wide range of managers at many different levels, *intelligence is irrelevant in determining who gets to*

177

the top. There are many things that do correlate with career success: clarity of purpose, drive and energy – yes, certainly; hard work – maybe. But intelligence is not one of them. Many intelligent people get nowhere – some remarkably unintelligent ones go a long way.

Many of the managers I meet refer to their careers with comments such as; 'Well, I'm enjoying my present job. I suppose, if they offer me a promotion I'll probably accept it, but I shan't worry if I don't get one.' Does that sound like someone who is on their way to the top? Clearly that will become a self-fulfilling prophecy.

Others, particularly women, having glimpsed the competitive atmosphere of many all-male board rooms, say: 'I don't want to join that sort of club' – but how else will change occur? Senior managers sometimes create an aura of power and infallibility; they hide behind big desks wearing smart suits, all of which can encourage a feeling of inferiority in others. When you get to know them as individuals, they are the same as anyone else. The rewards for the winners are colossal both in pay and satisfaction. Those senior managers who work 80-hour weeks do so not because they have to but because they enjoy it. You could get to the top if you want it enough, but you must set some clear objectives and there are sacrifices to be made.

If career success is not on your agenda (and it certainly won't be for everyone), it is still important to ask yourself what you want to get from your job, what you can contribute to it – and to set some clear objectives.

COMMUNITY GOALS

In our role as citizens we are all members of a broader community and we must ask ourselves what we can contribute to that community. As managers we have much to offer. If we opt out, then community life must suffer, which will be to our own ultimate disadvantage. In the USA, most managers are involved in multiple community activities. In the UK, many contribute little.

Making a contribution does not necessarily mean joining the local parent teachers association, whose interminable meetings seem to be the social highlight of the week for many, but thinking creatively about the skills you have to offer, and how those could be applied usefully in the community in some time-effective manner.

As we get older, we increasingly come to judge ourselves on what we have contributed to the lives of others. Those people I meet who have found some outlet for their energies and skills often report that it becomes a cornerstone of their lives and a highlight of their week. It brings them additional meaning and purpose.

What could you contribute to the community?

Values

We all have values which give meaning to our lives, make us part of humanity and determine that for which we will ultimately fight.

Values are the leverage points for the impulse to excel. They bring enthusiasm, commitment and astonishing energy to our actions: 'Give me a place to stand and I will move the earth.' Your place to stand must be your values, the things you truly believe in.

But what are they?

What are your values?

Who are you?

Few values are absolute. The values of our society in the 1990s are very different from those of the 1790s; the values of society in Britain differ from those of Japan, Iran and even France; your values will differ from those of other members of your community; and your own values may change through time.

What are your values?

The importance of values

There are no pressures greater than those which come from within; they colour our lives and influence our reaction to every situation.

We are happiest when we can live our values – when there is congruity between our actions and our values – and we suffer, sometimes consciously but more often subconsciously, when there is incongruity. The first step towards congruity must be to discover your own values. We all have values, but few people try to articulate them.

If asked for their values, most people describe a series of principles to which they aspire, or which they think they ought to live to, rather than the ones they actually use day by day. These principles were often absorbed early in our lives from parents, schools, the church or society. The chances are that those who 'taught' us were also articulating principles which they thought we ought to adopt rather than the ones they actually lived by. We accepted many of these ideas without question, building them into our subconscious mind-sets. Later in life we are sometimes dimly aware that our behaviour is falling short of these ideals. If we are not careful, this undermines our self-esteem and leaves us feeling guilty. As suggested earlier, self-esteem is a vital commodity and feeling guilty is a waste of time.

Everyone has, at some time, done something they have felt uncomfortable about. They then lose sleep, become irritable or feel stressed; they worry that they will be found out; they kick themselves for having done it. Whenever you feel like that, you have met one of your values. Dig it out; articulate it; test it. Do you truly believe in it? – in which case can you find a way of living by it? Or is it just a value you accepted unquestioningly but to which you are not committed? – in which case discard it.

We must discover our own values. For each of us there is a point at which we say, 'No ... that is wrong ... I won't do that.' We are all ethical beings at some level. We must discover our own true values, because they define who we are and self-concept is a major determinant of behaviour. Our main obligation in life is to be true to ourselves. We must learn to trust ourselves. With this inner core of certainty and comfort, we can cope with the uncertainties and unfairness of the world. When we define our ideal future we articulate our values, and when we discover our core values, we determine our preferred future and give ourselves permission to pursue it.

The next section consists of a series of exercises which might help in exploring your goals and values.

LIFE-GOALS AND VALUES

Exercise 1.

Draw a line for your life
1. Take a piece of paper, turn the long side to the bottom and mark a scale across the bottom to represent the years of your life, from 0 up to the present day and ten years into the future.
2. Draw a line to represent your life from birth to the present day. Presumably this line will have various ups and downs. Draw it now, before reading any further.

3. Label the peaks, the troughs, the turning points and any other significant features of your line.
4. Then (and not before) try to describe what you are measuring on the vertical scale.
5. Now project the line forward for ten years.
6. Finally, list the assumptions you have made in this forward projection.

Exercise 2.

Highlights of my life
1. Find a quiet place and reflect on your life in recent years. Which have been the periods of greatest satisfaction, happiness and motivation?
2. Choose one specific period when you felt very happy. Relax, close your eyes, try to recapture the tone and quality of that period.

- In what ways did you feel good?
- What effect did these feelings have on you?
- Who was associated with those good feelings?
- What else can you remember about those feelings?

3. When did you last experience those sorts of feelings?
4. What can you do to create such situations more often in the future?
5. Repeat the exercise again several times with other happy experiences. Try to explore a variety of work and non-work examples.

Exercise 3.

Write your own obituary
Newspapers prepare the obituaries of famous people while they are alive and well, and update them periodically.

1. Write your own obituary, setting it in the third person.
   Jan Neilsen was born . . .

Make it objective and factual, describing yourself only as seen by other people.

2. When you have completed the obituary, add a postscript. Assume that it is being written in 24 months' time – two years from today. What would you like to be able to write about those two years? (Continue to write in the third person and in the past tense.)

Exercise 4.

Investment analysis

You are being asked to invest in a business; you ask three questions.

- What will this business do?
  Answer: We're not sure yet. We haven't had time to decide.
- What are its strengths?
  Answer: Nothing special.
- What are its weaknesses?
  Answer: Oh lots! Too many to name.

Will you invest? The answer is yes, you are already investing. The business is you. Try those questions again:

- What are your strengths?
  What have you achieved in your life?
  What have you done that you are proud of?
  What were the strengths which contributed to those successes?
  List all the compliments you have received in recent years, whether deserved or not. (Don't be shy, this is for your own eyes only.)
- What are your weaknesses?
  What have been your failures?
  What have you done that has made you sad?
  What weaknesses contributed to these problems?
  List all the criticisms you have received, again whether reasonable or not.
- What business are you in?
- What are you going to do?

Exercise 5.

Dialogue with yourself

When you face a dilemma – when you are unsure how to choose between two different courses of action – imagine two different versions of yourself, each representing one course of action. You might imagine the ambitious career you and the home and family you; or the logical, rational you and the spontaneous emotional you; or, for dieting, the thin you and the self-indulgent you.

Get one of these characters to address the other (preferably in writing or on tape) and the other to respond. The dialogue will then develop.

You might be able to construct the dialogue at one sitting, or you might prefer to start with a lengthy input from your current state of mind and to delay the response until you feel in the appropriate mood. The process may take several weeks.

Educated people, especially men, tend to run from feeling and to hide behind theorizing and thinking, but the brain is clever, it deals in mind-sets and false logic which can imprison us. We never do anything well unless we *feel* like it, so emotions are powerful and *valuable*. Try to capture them: when you feel elated or frustrated, ask yourself why you care – and keep asking until you get to something that comes from the heart. Learn to listen to yourself and to observe your values changing through time.

Defining core values is tough; living them is harder. One who did this was Benjamin Franklin. After much consideration he arrived at a list of 12 values: temperance, silence, order, resolution, frugality, industry, sincerity, justice, moderation, cleanliness, tranquillity, chastity.

He subsequently added a thirteenth, humility. He is said to have concentrated on one value each day and to have reported that, just when he thought he had succeeded at the first twelve, the thirteenth would escape him.

PUT YOUR GOALS AND VALUES IN WRITING

How many diets do you have to go on to get thin?

How many times do you have to give up smoking?

It is not the plan that matters, it's the commitment. Make sure your goals are your own. Make sure you really want to achieve them. Write them down so that you can look at them regularly to remind yourself of what you are about, and always state them in positive terms: 'I will . . .' If you don't expect to achieve them, you won't.

Dream about them

We become what we think about. There is a lot of research evidence that time spent in mental rehearsal is one of the best forms of training. Most top athletes spend time imagining themselves breaking through the barrier, and people learning public speaking imagine themselves speaking well in public. Allow yourself to dream, regularly, about the achievement of your objectives. There is an old Spanish proverb: 'If you build no castles in the air you build no castles anywhere.'

Life is a marathon, not a sprint

TV is full of happy endings – life is not, but it is the complexity of life that makes it so much fun.

Some objectives are achievable, they are stepping stones along the road – others are more distant, they give us direction and a basis for decision-taking.

The marathon runners are aware of their objective, but focus their attention on the process of running, which brings us to the subject of planning.

24. *Strategic Planning*

PLANNING FOR THE ACHIEVEMENT OF OBJECTIVES

Ancient Chinese proverb: 'It is not enough to come to the river intending to fish, you have to bring a net.'

An objective without a plan is just a dream. No *organization* would agree its objectives and fail to plan for their achievement – yet many *people* do just that.

I've just found some of your dreams and ambitions.
Can I throw them out now?

Imagine yourself walking by a canal. As you round a corner you see a child fall into the water, obviously in trouble. Nobody else is in sight. I suggest you would have no hesitation in running to the child and doing everything you could to save it, jumping into the water yourself if necessary. You certainly wouldn't procrastinate. Why?

- The objective is clear
- The action needed is obvious
- You know that you are accountable
- The outcome is predictable
- The feedback will be immediate

This, then, is the recipe for action; the formula for planning. The purpose of planning is to make it easy to act in pursuit of an objective. 'I want to improve my French' may be a very worthy objective, but it doesn't tell me what I should do tomorrow. Surely the first step I should take is to decide whether to join an evening class, buy a tape or spend time in France. Until I've done that nothing will happen. Every plan should consist of a clear objective and a series of actions, each of which should be:

- Clearly identifiable
- Measurable
- With a timescale
- With milestones to check progress
- With feedback loops

We tend to neglect some of our major objectives, both at home and at work, because they are too large and we don't know where to begin. This makes it easy to find reasons for postponing them.

Most managers derive a lot of their motivation from a sense of achievement. You will increase your chances of achieving your own objectives if you break each one down into a series of practical stages. What are you actually going to do, step by step, in pursuit of that objective?

Since deadlines tend to dictate priorities and engender a sense of urgency, each stage in the plan should be given a deadline. When are you going to do it? And each must be measurable, with a performance standard. In other words, how will you know whether you have achieved it? The satisfaction derived from measuring your progress against such a plan can provide valuable reinforcement of your resolution.

Many of the managers I meet are good at setting objectives, but seem to have trouble with the process of action planning. The following sample action plan illustrates the process and is deliberately set in the context of a personal objective to show how the process can be applied in any area. The objective is one which many people struggle with unsuccessfully: losing weight.

ACTION PLAN
Objective: Lose 20 lbs in weight within six months.

Action:	Timescale:
1. Read three different books on diet, exercise, health.	By the end of this month.
2. Construct a diet and exercise plan.	By the end of this month.
3. Purchase some reliable bathroom scales.	By the end of this month.
4. Weigh myself every day and record the weight, against a target of losing 1 lb per week.	Daily.
5. On any day when my weight exceeds the target, stick rigidly to the diet and exercise plan.	Daily, as necessary.
6. Review progress and set a new objective.	In six months' time.

That is not fool proof, nothing is fool proof. But the biggest problem many people face in trying to lose weight is that they cheat. What this plan does is to set a clear daily target and feedback loop. It makes it harder to hide.

There is an interesting parallel between losing weight and time management. Why do we put on weight? Well, our metabolisms play a part, but beyond that we put on weight because we give way to many small pleasures during the day and lose sight of our longer-term objective. That is exactly the problem we face in managing our time.

Why do we decide to lose weight? Because we don't like what we see in the mirror, or are worried by the risk to our health. In time management the mirror is the time log and the recognition of our potential, of what we would achieve if we made better use of our time.

The good news is that, whereas losing weight involves giving up all the little pleasures for a considerable time before we start to see the results, with time management the results can be seen much more quickly.

When someone succeeds in controlling their weight, nobody believes they have a problem. People express great surprise when they decline food or drink for reasons of weight. People often seem to assume that you can't have a problem *unless you fail to control it*. Is the same true with your time? Will you find ways of controlling it better and achieving your objectives? Or will you just make a lot of noise about it and do nothing?

The process of action planning should be applied to each of your major objectives, like organizing your desk and work area, learning a language, improving your communication skills, or learning to use a Personal Organizer.

At the end of this chapter is a simple form which you can use to draw up an action plan for one objective.

FORCE-FIELD ANALYSIS

At the planning stage some objectives seem so obvious that their attainment appears simple. Regrettably this is seldom the case. In addition to the problem of our own mind-sets and habits, we must deal with those of other people. Our lives are enmeshed with others, at work as well as at home, and any change you make will have an impact on them. People and organizations tend to resist change, especially when they don't understand it, and the deathly forces of 'Status Quo' can smother much fresh enthusiasm.

Kurt Lewin's technique of force-field analysis can be a useful tool in planning for change. It involves taking one single objective, preferably one that is very important to you, and writing it as clearly and concisely as you can at the top of a sheet of paper. (Another simple form at the end of this chapter can be copied for this purpose.)

Whatever your objective, there are likely to be a number of forces or factors which might hinder its achievement. Think creatively about these, brainstorm them, writing them down in any order. Try to find at least ten.

They may include people who will resist you, people who might have to do more work as a result, lack of information on your part, lack of time and some aspects of your own personal character which might tempt you back into the comfortable old ways.

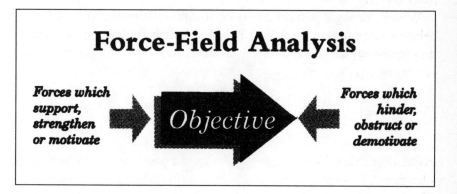

Force-Field Analysis

Forces which support, strengthen or motivate

Objective

Forces which hinder, obstruct or demotivate

If, as part of your objective, you plan to change your behaviour in relation to another person, what could be their initial reaction? For example, if you have tended to be a bit autocratic and now intend to be more consultative and participative, the person may initially see this as being manipulative.

List all these possible obstacles – as many as you can. Then, quite separately, work your way down the list focusing on each potential obstacle in turn, and asking:

- How can I weaken that force?
- How can I avoid that obstacle?
- How can I make sure that factor does not prevent my reaching that objective?

Then list all the forces which will support and strengthen your intentions, again being creative. Who are the people who could be supportive and who will want you to succeed? What are the pay-offs for success? What aspect of your own character and motivation will help? Go through the list, item by item, asking yourself:

- How can I reinforce that force?
- How can I make sure that force brings maximum support to me when I need it?

Force-field analysis is a laborious process, but if it is thoroughly conducted and the results built into an action plan, it is a very powerful method of increasing dramatically your chances of achieving your chosen objective.

All this strategic planning may seem like hard work, and it is. But, like budgeting, it is an occasional task which will steer and guide many months of activity.

ACTION PLANNING

Use this sheet to develop an action plan for one important objective.

Objective		
Actions Each clearly identifiable and measurable	**Date for Completion**	**Review comments** Remember, no excuses
1.		
2.		
3.		
4.		
5.		
6.		
7.		
8.		
9.		
10.		

FORCE-FIELD ANALYSIS

Choose an objective which is very important to you, but which might be difficult to achieve.

Objective:	
Factors which might hinder, obstruct or demotivate.	**Strategies to get round them or weaken them.**
1.	
2.	
3.	
4.	
5.	
6.	
7.	
8.	
9.	
10.	
Factors which will support, strengthen and motivate.	**Strategies to reinforce them.**
1.	
2.	
3.	
4.	
5.	
6.	

25. Tactical Planning

WHAT SHALL I DO TODAY?

The previous chapter was about planning for the achievement of major objectives. This one is about planning the day, the week and the month.

Objectives can be set for any timescale: daily, annual, even lifetime objectives. Planning must be on a shorter timescale. It would be unrealistic for most of us to plan a year ahead in detail. You might have a lifetime objective, but the detailed plans should address the question: 'What am I going to do this week to move me down the road in the direction of that objective?'

Any time-planning system should be flexible. It should be designed to suit you personally. It must not become a treadmill or a problem, but a tool which you can enjoy using. Because each system must be personally designed, I shall take you through the system I have evolved for myself and explain why I use it in the way I do.

I use three timescales for planning: they are approximately a year, a month and a day. These could be called long-term, medium-term and short-term plans. Three separate sets of plans will seem excessive to action-oriented readers, but they have come to seem natural to me.

Long-Term Plans

I know I just said that you cannot plan a year ahead in detail, and I stand by that. My annual plan is a very rough outline. Early in November I take stock of the next year. I note any significant commitments, such as course tutorships; I decide when to take my principal holiday; and I choose a few major objectives for the year, such as writing a book, developing a new programme, or learning French. I then construct my strategic plans for the achievement of these major objectives.

The whole process takes only an hour or two. It is very rough and ready, but it gives me an overview of the year ahead.

Medium-Term Plans

This is where the real time-planning starts. I don't work to calendar months, I tend to work to the next natural break point in my diary, such as Christmas, Easter, a long holiday or overseas trip, or a course tutorship. The medium-term plans thus tend to be for four to eight weeks.

I set up a sheet for the period in my organizer and start by writing down all my appointments and firm commitments. Then I calculate roughly the amount of discretionary time that is left – that is, time not already committed. I calculate in terms of half-days, counting mornings and afternoons separately.

Then I deduct from that the time I expect to need for routine administration and correspondence and all the other things that fill up the 'to do' list (about one hour per day or five per week) and for routine reading (also an hour per day or five per week).

That might leave me with, let's say, five mornings and three after-noons still free in a month. Now comes the exciting bit. I work through my organizer and list all the major activities that I *must* undertake and all the activities I would like to undertake and I prepare my monthly time budget. As with all budgets there are always far more candidates for expenditure than there is time avail-able and I must pare down the list until it looks realistic.

The final stage of the medium-term plan is to book the most important items into my diary. It is at this point that I book any free mornings for my high-concentration tasks, though all diary entries are in pencil. I am also careful to book in planning time. For example, at least a week before any teaching commitment I reserve time to plan the session and collect the material. A week before writing a paper, I reserve time to gather all the necessary informa-tion together.

Short-Term Plans

These are normally daily plans, though it sometimes seems appro-priate to plan two or three days together. As an early riser, I like to get up knowing what I am going to do and get on with it quickly, so I always plan a day at the end of the previous day.

Once again I start with any firm commitments, such as appointments. I assess the minimum time I will need to keep my 'to do' list under control, and I then select a high-leverage task from the medium-term plan.

In scheduling the day, I am very conscious of my natural daily cycle. For all of us there is a natural cycle to the day: there are times of day when we tend to feel bright and alert, and there are times when we tend to feel sluggish. Hours must be measured by quality as well as by quantity. Most people follow a fairly similar pattern. In the early hours of the morning, our potential for performance is very low. Even if you are wide awake at 3.00a.m., your brain is unlikely to be fully functional. Anyone who has tried to drive through the night on holiday knows that.

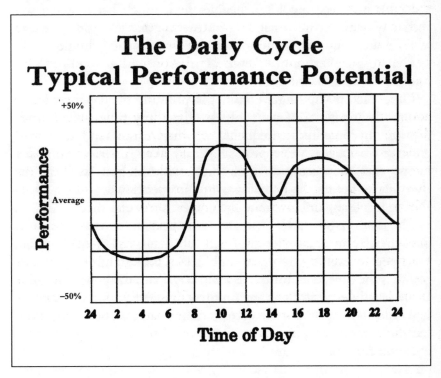

Then the body systems start to wake up before we reach consciousness. Some wake faster than others; I reckon I reach my peak of efficiency by about 7.00a.m. and then go downhill all day after that! Others start more slowly, but most of us reach our peak during the morning.

There is a pronounced dip after lunch. In part this has to do with the body systems concentrating on digesting food, but I find that the post-lunch dip occurs even when I don't eat. Maybe the siesta is a natural part of the daily cycle.

During the afternoon our potential rises again, but most people don't quite reach the level of the morning peak and potential performance gradually tails away during the evening. After a couple of glasses of wine I sometimes think I am working well in the evening, but the results are usually not so good when I re-examine them in the morning. There are some people who can do their best work late in the evening, but I think they are few.

What matters is that you are aware of your own daily cycle and plan round it. I always try to schedule high-concentration tasks for the mornings, because I can handle them much better and faster then. My secretary has a standing instruction that if anyone wants to arrange a meeting or a routine teaching session she should try to steer it to an afternoon. Likewise I try to avoid all routine, low-brainpower tasks in the mornings.

Other factors you might consider in planning the day include the natural daily pattern of your job. Are there any times when interruptions become more frequent, or when crises tend to occur? Anyone working in a European subsidiary of an American company knows that they must do their high-concentration work in the mornings – before the E-mails start to shower down.

Straight lines and accurate schedules occur in theory and in mechanization, but rarely in reality, for managers. It is a mistake to plan the day in detail, because such schedules will frequently fail. Unexpected events may occur and claim your attention. The daily plan sets the objectives for the day and lays down the preferred route. If the schedule is too tight any unforeseen event will lead to failure. It should allow space for the occasional diversion without jeopardizing the end objectives.

If you find that you are frequently failing to complete your daily plan it is important to analyse why. Are you trying to plan too much of the day? In some jobs you might only be able to plan for one or two hours per day. An easy schedule kept is far better than a demanding one missed. Are you consistently under-estimating the time needed to complete tasks? This can be a serious problem because it tempts you to accept more tasks than you should and it leads to unrealistic plans. Where plans are unrealistic, the urgent will squeeze out the important. If you are consistently under-estimating the time needed for low-leverage tasks, you should find a way of avoiding more of them, and ensure that you complete the others within the scheduled time. Beware the trap of perfectionism.

Are you over-committed? This is a common problem of poor time managers, and over-commitment of time has much the same result as financial over-commitment. In the words of Mr Micawber:

Annual income £20, annual expenditure 19 pounds, 19 shillings and sixpence – result happiness.

Annual income £20, annual expenditure 20 pounds and sixpence – result misery. (*David Copperfield*, Charles Dickens.)

Are you procrastinating? If so, take comfort from the fact that you are not severely disabled by the disease – the worst cases are planning to start reading this book tomorrow. But do something about it.

A successful life is a succession of successful days, and a successful day usually starts with a plan. Without a plan, chaos will reign.

Specific Plans

Planning is a vital component of efficiency in other dimensions as well. If you had to drive to a town you didn't know, you wouldn't jump into the car and start driving (I hope), you would look at a map and plan the journey. Likewise it is well worth your while to take a few moments to plan before chairing a meeting, writing a report, conducting an interview, making a phone call, and in countless other situations.

Ask yourself:

- What do I need for this task?
- What do I want to achieve?
- How much time should I allow for it?
- What can I do to make the most of the opportunity?

Again and again, five minutes spent planning can save ten minutes of activity time and can greatly reduce the risk of getting lost, wasting the meeting or forgetting to ask that key question. Successful executives spend time planning and then follow through calmly and efficiently.

Punctuality

Are you always on time for appointments and meetings?

I used to think I was making good use of my time by working right up to the very last moment, until I read that those who are frequently late are either: naughty children drawing attention to themselves; exercising power over others by delaying them; or livening up a dull life with a game of 'will I miss my plane?'

If punctuality is the courtesy of kings, maybe tardiness is the sport of the unhappy. Better to go in good time and take something to read while you wait.

26. Personal Organizers

All managers have systems for organizing themselves. They have project plans, checklists, reminder lists, records of expenses, messages, notes taken at meetings and so on – often on scraps of paper, which can occasionally go astray.

Some people report that the Personal Organizer, either in book form or electronic, has changed their lives, that it enables them to achieve far more than they ever could before. Such people have almost invariably extended the system for use in organizing their private lives as well as their work – and could not now contemplate life without one.

Far more people, however, have spent large sums of money on a sophisticated system which they use only as an appointment diary, or which is sitting gathering dust on their desk and conscience.

There seem to be considerable problems associated with these systems: the book tends to be big and bulky and it doesn't fit easily into a handbag or briefcase; if you lose it you are in serious trouble; it can come to dominate your life; less sophisticated and badly organized people rationalize their failure by making jokes about them; and worst of all, it seems to be very difficult to learn how to use it effectively. There is a long and painful learning curve.

Some non-users say that they don't want to be 'boring and organized', they want to be more spontaneous. That is a serious misconception: organization doesn't constrict, it liberates. It is only when you are properly organized that you can create the space for spontaneity and creativity. It is the disorganized people who tend to be under pressure and therefore never have time for anything.

Some people are by nature systematic and organized (did I hear someone say boring?). They will usually find it easy to adapt to a

*A Personal Organizer can
come to dominate your life*

Personal Organizer; if they also happen to be boring, this stems from their nature and not their use of the system.

Other people are by nature more creative and disorganized. They would stand to gain far more from learning to use a Personal Organizer but, because of their nature, they will experience far greater difficulty in mastering the system. When they succeed, they will find that the system will aid and channel their creativity, not stifle it. If you were to persuade the Marketing Director to wear the

Chief Accountant's suit, would that make him boring? Of course not! Give up this excuse!

Personal Organizers have, perforce, been designed by organized people. They are, therefore, quite sophisticated, complex and difficult to use. (Experts everywhere tend to make their subjects difficult for the general public.) But using a Personal Organizer is a skill, like speaking French, driving a car or playing badminton – and skills can be learned by anyone.

A Personal Organizer is a system for organizing yourself, a portable office. Like time management generally, it should not become a treadmill or an end in itself, but a tool to serve you, to lead you towards greater effectiveness and efficiency, and thus to reduce your stress.

There are basically two ways to get started.

The first is the 'big bang approach'. You spend two full days setting up all the sub-systems, probably by attending a special course; you reorganize your entire life to fit the system dictated by the publisher; you then force yourself to use it every day for every-thing; and you go through six months of agony as you gradually get used to it.

The other approach is to start simply by transferring your exist-ing systems into an organizer; then to draw up an action plan to develop your systems gradually over an extended period, probably at least a year. You might plan to set up one new system at the start of each month and to spend the month developing and refining that system and learning to use it efficiently. This approach lessens the pain and confusion, but extends the time needed to learn.

Whichever route you choose, you should be ready to adapt the systems to suit yourself, so that they can in due course become a pleasure to use. You must also set yourself clear performance standards for routine maintenance – up-dating systems, filing items systematically and throwing out pages wherever possible. It would be easy but disastrous to add a cluttered Organizer to a cluttered desk.

But be warned: the learning curve is a long one, especially if you are the sort of person who really needs one. Don't embark on this exercise until you are sufficiently committed to persist, to get through the pain threshold and reach the promised land of organized serenity.

WHAT TO PUT IN THE ORGANIZER

You must design your own system. But people often ask me what to put in, so here are some suggestions:

Strategy section
- Job description
- Major objectives – personal, family and community as well as work – and each with an action plan. I also have a page for each major area of responsibility and a page for each major client
- Outline plan for the year
- Medium-term plan for the month ahead, which is drawn largely from the strategy sections

Planning section
- Reminder or 'to do' list, to keep track of all the little jobs you must do, most of which don't have dates or times attached to them. Everything is written down, thus simultaneously reducing the risk of losing anything and clearing the mind of trivial clutter
- Daily plan – this can be constructed at the end of the previous day and drawn from diary commitments, your medium-term plan and your 'to do' list
- A notable absentee from this section is a diary. Personally, I find it easier to use a pocket diary for appointments

Data bank
- Telephone numbers and addresses
- Checklists for standard jobs
- Record of expenses
- Any other information you might need

Notes
- A scrap pad for notes
- An ideas page, where you can jot down bright ideas that occur while driving, watching TV or listening to boring speakers
- A memory page for interesting or amusing things you have heard or read which you want to remember. I often glance at this section to cheer me up while waiting for people who can't keep to time – like doctors, dentists and British trains

If you are going to proceed, I suggest that you talk to one or two experts, people who already use one comprehensively. Most people who have mastered the system are only too pleased to show it to a keen learner and to offer advice.

FACT: Most successful people, including the highly creative, have a well-developed system of organization, usually based on a Personal Organizer.

27. Reviewing

If you have set some objectives, drawn up your plans and started to implement them, the final stage in the cycle is the review. Progress must be measured regularly against plans and budgets.

In organizations, managers have no sooner completed their budgets than the accountants are back again:

'This is what you said you would do.'

'This is what you have actually done.'

'This is the variance. Please explain it.'

That is an awful nuisance. It is much more fun making things or selling things, but even marketing managers recognize that the process is essential. Progress must be measured regularly against plans and budgets. It is the control mechanism that enables managers to keep an organization on course. We all know what happens to organizations with weak control and feedback systems.

I believe that the same is true for each person as an individual. Having objectives and plans is not enough; there must be a regular formal review of progress against those plans if you are to stay on course. Be too lenient with yourself here and you will miss out.

We are all very quick to judge other people on their behaviour, but each of us is inclined to judge ourselves on our *intentions*. That is not enough. Without regular formal reviews we learn very slowly. Experience alone is a poor teacher – the main thing we learn from experience is the type of mistakes we will go on making throughout our lives, or, as Oscar Wilde put it, 'The joy of making a mistake is that you recognize it when you make it again.'

Sales people are taught this. Before every call, set a clear objective. Before every call draw up a plan. And *after* every call, spend a few minutes (in a stationary car not a moving one) reviewing your performance:

● What did I do well?

- What did I do badly?
- How could I have handled it better?
- What can I do to make sure I do better next time?

All sales managers know that this is the way to learn. All sales managers teach this to their people. Every sales person knows this: few of them practise it regularly. But the best ones do, and that is how they became the best.

Nobody could become an expert at selling, or at any other skill, by attending a single course, however good the programme. What is needed is a great deal of practice, combined with a systematic analysis of performance and a method of feeding this back into future objective setting and planning.

Could you discipline yourself to spend five minutes at the end of each day reviewing your performance against your plan? It would provide a powerful ratchet mechanism for improving your performance slowly and steadily over a period of time. Review your performance by asking yourself:

- What did I set out to do today?
- What did I actually do?
- What is the variance? And why?
- I will never have that day again. Did I spend it well?
- Can I learn any lessons from it?

It is often surprising to discover how much we know if we ask ourselves instead of someone else.

The same procedure can be applied on different timescales and different occasions. You can review your performance at the end of a project, meeting or interview. You can also conduct the occasional spontaneous review in the middle of the working day:

- Why am I doing this task?
- How well do I need to do it?
- If I had to complete it in half the time, what would I do?

Without formal reviews it is too easy to get stuck in a rut and then to slip into the 'loser' frame of mind – and that is very hard to spot in the heat of the action.

Picture the scene: Tony is driving to work. The day has started badly. The children were arguing at breakfast, the toast got burnt, and he is already running late. He has an 8.30a.m. meeting and is having to drive rather faster than usual to get there.

Suddenly he sees a red Porsche, overtaking. It squeezes in front of him and he has to ease back slightly to let it in. Tony feels his blood pressure rising. In an instant he has changed down to second gear and put his headlights full on; his heart is pumping fast and he is driving three feet away from the Porsche. Whose problem is that?

'Mine? You must be joking! Didn't you see the stupid way he drove?' There is no way Tony's ego will let him take a balanced view – at least, not in the heat of the moment.

But what if Tony was to take a few minutes at the end of the day for a cool, calm, objective appraisal:

- What did I set out to do today?
- What did I actually do?

And maybe the third question should be:

- What could I have done differently to have achieved a better outcome for me?

There is a small chance that he will manage to say to himself: 'Ah! I have a problem, I get over-excited by things that don't matter very much. I must do something about that.' Then he might learn. You cannot solve any problem until you recognize it and accept it as *your* problem. People seldom get angry for the reason they think they are angry: the review session is a time for personal honesty, an opportunity to make an objective analysis of your own performance. We all know other people who keep making the same mistakes, who seem to go round in circles. In the words of Robert Burns:

> O wad some Power the giftie gie us
> To see oursels as others see us!
> It wad frae monie a blunder free us
> An' foolish notion

This formal review is as close as we can get to answering Burns's plea. It is a form of appraisal interview, and like all appraisal interviews it is much easier and more effective to appraise against clear objectives. Many people see the events of the day as blessings or curses. Successful people see them as challenges and opportunities.

When you fail or feel unhappy, analyse why. Search for the attitudes, habits and mind-sets that are causing the problem. Our instinct is to shy away from such tensions and emotions, worried that we might discover something nasty. But tension and emotion are signs of life and an opportunity for learning. They give us clues to our real values. Every situation is a learning opportunity.

Life is a series of choices. On each occasion we can choose the easy comfortable path, or we can opt for growth. Notice what excites you and what irritates you. Analyse why. Even destructive emotions like fear and anger can be managed. The review is not just for failures, it is equally for reflecting on successes. We work best when we feel good about ourselves, so recognize your successes and wallow in them. It is quite possible to revel in a success without becoming complacent. Analyse your strengths and skills so that you can make even better use of them in the future.

If you read the biographies of successful people, you will probably be struck by how often they had to overcome colossal handicaps early in their lives. It was through overcoming those hardships that they became winners and gained the self-confidence that took them on to future success.

Whenever you hear yourself playing a 'loser tape' ('it's not my fault'), stop and think how you can change it to a 'winner tape'. *You* can decide, in every situation, which tape to play. *You* can decide whether to be a winner or a loser. Just as the words of the loser tape make you a loser, so the words of a winner tape may help:

I am responsible for myself.
I choose the feelings I experience, and their strength.
I decide my goals, and how hard to chase them.
I control my own time and my own life.

28. The End of the Book and the Beginning of the Action?

Most of us don't lead well-planned lives. We live day by day, reacting to the pressures and temptations of the moment. Our lives are a battle between order and chaos: on good days we take charge and get organized; on bad days we sink back into busyness. Not having time absorbs all available energy and leaves us feeling stressed. It becomes a way of life and an excuse for failures. We spin round in circles for a few grains of psychological corn, bolstering our egos with a series of shallow victories.

'Like Gulliver, among the Lilliputians, tied down by a multitude of subtle bonds, none of which is individually strong enough to immobilize us but which together deprive us of our freedom.' (Jean-Louis Servan-Schreiber.)

It is generally recognized that for an organization to achieve profits, it must stop focusing on the short term and the bottom line and concentrate, instead, on quality. It is equally true that, to achieve quality, people must move their focus from the products they produce to the processes of production. And to achieve happiness and self-confidence we must stop focusing on our egos and concentrate instead on our goals and values.

To manage time we must take our eyes off the clock and focus on tasks and priorities. This does not mean working longer, it may not mean working harder – it means working more *systematically*. It means being cleverer and smarter at allocating time and effort more precisely. It means setting clear objectives and planning to achieve them. So what are you going to do about it?

After five chapters on the planning cycle, perhaps I should now redress the balance by repeating the words of Peter Drucker: 'Planning is of no use at all unless it eventually degenerates into work.' Add to that John Lennon's 'Life is what happens while you're making other plans.' Planning is a preliminary, it carries the planner nowhere. Life is about *doing*. So what are you going to *do*?

Given the difficulty we all face in changing our patterns of behaviour, I always invite seminar participants to make a public commitment to change: name one thing you will do which has in some way been stimulated by this seminar. All too often the responses I get are something like:

- I'm going to try to organize my desk
- I want to improve my reading skills
- I intend to start each day with a plan
- I hope to delegate more

My reply to answers like these is that trying, wanting, intending and hoping are *noisy ways of doing nothing*: either you will organise your desk, or you won't. Which is it to be? Wishing is fishing without a hook. There is no room on the scoreboard for trying.

Every time you set an objective and fail, you diminish your self-image and reduce your chances of success next time. Mediocrity becomes a habit. If you fail often enough you will rationalize this by rubbishing the planning process.

Conversely, every time you set an objective and succeed, you raise your self-image and increase your chances of future success.

This suggests that you should take great care in setting objectives. Don't be over-ambitious; far better to make just one successful permanent change to your system per month than to try ten and fail at eight. Habits, like muscles, strengthen with use.

Take charge of your time and you take charge of your life.

> This is the time
> This is the place
> This is your life
> This is your opportunity to influence your future
> Seize this day
> Use this moment
> Act now

Bibliography

Black, R., (1988) *Getting Things Done*, London: Michael Joseph.

Buzan, T., (1988) *Use Your Head*, London: BBC Books.

Buzan, T., (1989) *Make the Most of Your Mind*, London: Pan.

Handy, C., (1991) *Gods of Management*, London: Century Business.

Harvey-Jones, J., (1988) *Making it Happen*, London: Collins.

Imai, M., (1986) *Kaizen: The Key to Japan's Competitive Success*, New York: McGraw Hill.

De Leeuw, M. and E., (1965) *Read Better, Read Faster*, London: Penguin.

Ohmae, K., (1990) *The Borderless World*, London: Collins.

Oncken, W., Jnr, (1984) *Managing Management Time*, New Jersey: Prentice-Hall.

Porter, M.E., (1990) *The Competitive Advantage of Nations*, London: Macmillan.

Servan-Schrieber, J-L., (1989) *The Art of Time*, London: Bloomsbury.

Tannen, D., (1991) *You Just Don't Understand* London: Virago.

Thomson, K., (1990) *The Employee Revolution*, London: Pitman.

Index